Don't Forget to Write

Your experiences—positive and negative—matter to us. If we have missed or misstated something, we want to hear about it. We follow up on all suggestions. Contact the New Mexico editor at editors@fodors.com or c/o Fodor's at 1745 Broadway, New York, NY 10019. And have a fabulous trip!

Karen Cure
Editorial Director

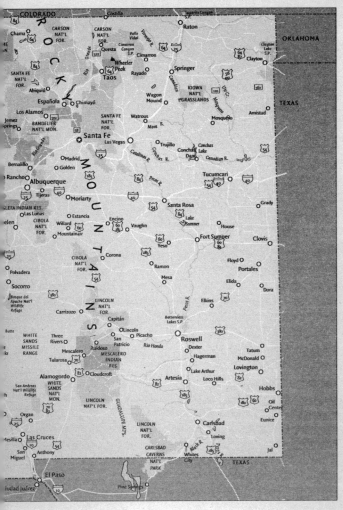

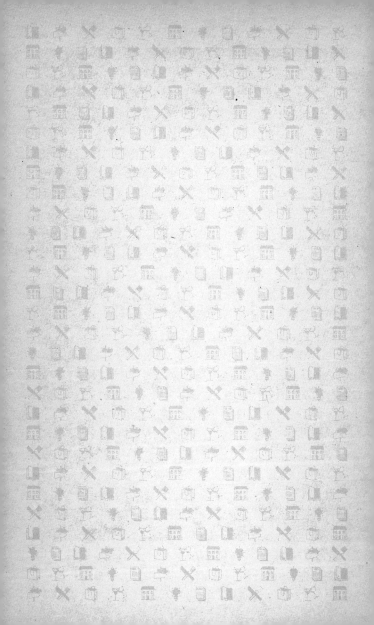

santa fe
and taos

In This Chapter

introducing santa fe and taos

NEW MEXICO'S TAGLINE is more than a marketing cliché. The state is truly a "Land of Enchantment," and Santa Fe is indisputably "the City Different." Surrounded by mind-expanding mountain views and filled with sinuous streets that discourage car traffic but invite leisurely exploration, Santa Fe welcomes with characteristic warmth, if not some trepidation. Rapid growth and development have taken their toll, prompting many local residents to worry about becoming too much like "everywhere else," and you'll hear various complaints about encroaching commercialism and its attendant T-shirt shops and fast-food restaurants that interfere with the rhythms of life here.

But despite (or perhaps, occasionally, because of) a surfeit of trendy restaurants, galleries, and boutiques that tout regional fare and wares, both authentic and artificial, Santa Fe remains a special place to visit. Commercialism notwithstanding, its deeply spiritual aura affects even nonreligious types in surprising ways, inspiring a reverence probably not unlike that which inspired the Spanish monks to name it "the City of Holy Faith." (Its full name is La Villa Real de la Santa Fe de San Francisco de Asís, or the Royal City of the Holy Faith of St. Francis of Assisi.) A kind of mystical Catholicism blended with ancient Native American lore and beliefs flourishes throughout northern New Mexico in tiny mountain villages that have seen little change through the centuries. Tales of miracles, spontaneous healings, and spiritual visitations thrive in the old adobe churches that line the High Road that leads north of Santa Fe to Taos.

If Santa Fe is spiritual, sophisticated, and occasionally superficial, Taos, 65 mi away, is very much an outpost despite its relative proximity to the capital. Compared with Santa Fe, Taos is smaller, feistier, quirkier, tougher, and very independent. Taoseños are a study in contradictions: Wary of strangers and suspicious of outsiders, they nevertheless accept visitors with genuine warmth and pride. Rustic and delightfully unpretentious, the town contains a handful of upscale restaurants with cuisines and wine lists as innovative as what you might find in New York. It's a haven for aging hippies, creative geniuses, cranky misanthropes, and anyone else who wants a good quality of life in a place that accepts new arrivals without a lot of questions—as long as they don't offend longtime residents with their city attitudes.

Unifying these towns and the terrain around them is the appeal of the land and the people. It's the character of the residents and their attitude toward the land that imbue New Mexico with its enchanted spirit. First-time visitors discover the unexpected pleasures of a place where time is measured not by linear calculations of hours, days, weeks, and years but in a circular sweep of crop cycles, gestation periods, the rotation of generations, and the changing of seasons.

PLEASURES AND PASTIMES

DINING

New Mexico's cuisine is a delicious and extraordinary mixture of Pueblo, Spanish colonial, and Mexican and American frontier cooking. Recipes that came from Spain via Mexico were adapted for local ingredients—chiles, corn, pork, wild game, pinto beans, honey, apples, and piñon nuts—and have remained much the same ever since.

In Santa Fe and Taos, babies cut their teeth on fresh flour tortillas and quickly develop a taste for sopaipillas, deep-fried, puff-pastry pillows, drizzled with honey. But it is the chile pepper, whether red or green, that is the heart and soul of northern New Mexican cuisine. You might be a bit surprised to learn that ristras, those strings of bright red chiles that seem to hang everywhere, are sold more for eating here than for decoration. More varieties of chiles—upward of 90—are grown in New Mexico than anywhere else in the world.

In most restaurants you can dress as casually as you like. Those in the major business hotels tend to be a bit more formal, but as the evening wears down, so do the restrictions.

OUTDOOR ACTIVITIES AND SPORTS

Canoeing and River Rafting

You can challenge yourself on New Mexico's rivers. The Taos Box, a 17-mi run through the churning rapids of the Rio Grande, is one of America's most exciting rafting experiences.

Golf

With several dozen courses, the state has a respectable share of turf, and the dry climate makes playing very comfortable. There are excellent public courses in Santa Fe and Taos.

Horse Racing

Horse racing with pari-mutuel betting is very popular in New Mexico. One of the more favored of the state's tracks is Downs at Santa Fe, 5 mi south of town.

Skiing

New Mexico contains many world-class downhill ski areas. Snowmaking equipment is used in most areas to ensure a long season, usually from Thanksgiving through Easter. The Santa Fe Ski Area averages 250 inches of dry-powder snow a year; it accommodates all levels of skiers on more than 40 trails. Within a 90-mi radius of Taos are resorts with slopes for all levels of skiers, as well as snowmobile and cross-country ski trails. The Taos Ski Valley resort is recognized internationally for its challenging terrain and European-style ambience.

PARKS AND MONUMENTS

New Mexico's state-park network includes nearly four dozen parks, ranging from high-mountain lakes and pine forests in the north to the Chihuahuan Desert lowlands of the south. Parks and monuments close to Santa Fe include Pecos National Historic Park and Jemez State Monument. The Carson National Forest is near Taos.

RESERVATIONS AND PUEBLOS

New Mexico's Pueblo cultures, each with its own reservation, and distinct but overlapping history, art, and customs, evolved out of the highly civilized Anasazi culture that built Chaco Canyon. Pueblos dating back centuries are located near Santa Fe and Taos; the best time to visit them is during one of their many year-round public dance ceremonies. Admission is free to pueblos unless otherwise indicated. Donations, however, are always welcome.

The pueblos around Santa Fe—San Ildefonso, Nambé, Pojoaque, and Santa Clara—are more infused with Spanish culture than are the pueblos in other areas. Dwellers here also have the keenest business sense when dealing with the sale of handicrafts and art and with matters touristic. The famous Taos Pueblo, unchanged through the centuries, is the personification of classic Pueblo Native American culture. It and the Picurís Pueblo near Taos have first-rate recreational facilities.

When visiting pueblos and reservations, you're expected to follow a certain etiquette. Each pueblo has its own regulations for the use of still and video cameras and video and tape recorders, as well as for sketching and painting. Some pueblos prohibit photography altogether. Others, such as Santa Clara, prohibit photography at certain times, such as during ritual dances. Still others allow photography but require a permit, which usually costs about $5 or $10 for a still camera. The privilege of setting up an easel and painting all day will cost you as little as $35 or as much as $150 (at Taos Pueblo). Be sure to ask permission before photographing anyone in the pueblos; it's also customary to give the subject a dollar or two for agreeing to be photographed. Native American law prevails on the pueblos, and violations of photography regulations could result in confiscation of cameras.

Specific restrictions for the various pueblos are noted in the individual descriptions. Other rules are described below.

- Possessing or using drugs and/or alcohol on Native American land is forbidden.

- Ritual dances often have serious religious significance and should be respected as such. Silence is mandatory—that means no questions about ceremonies or dances while they're being performed. Don't walk across the dance plaza during a performance, and don't applaud afterward.

- Kiva and ceremonial rooms are restricted to pueblo members only.

- Cemeteries are sacred. They're off-limits to all visitors and should never be photographed.

- Unless pueblo dwellings are clearly marked as shops, don't wander or peek inside. Remember, these are private homes.

Many of the pueblo buildings are hundreds of years old. Don't try to scale adobe walls or climb on top of buildings, or you may come tumbling down.

Don't litter. Nature is sacred on the pueblos, and defacing land can be a serious offense.

SHOPPING

Antiques

You'll find everything in New Mexico's shops, from early Mexican typewriters to period saddles, ceramic pots, farm tools, pioneer aviation equipment, and yellowed newspaper clippings about Kit Carson and D. H. Lawrence.

Art

Santa Fe, with more than 150 galleries, is the arts capital of the Southwest and a leading arts center nationally. Taos is not far behind. Native American art, Western art, Hispanic art, contemporary art, sculpture, photography, prints, ceramics, jewelry, folk art, junk art—it's all for sale in New Mexico, produced by artists of international and local renown.

Crafts

Hispanic handcrafted furniture and *santos* (saints) command high prices from collectors. Santos are religious carvings and paintings in the form of *bultos* (three-dimensional carvings) and *retablos* (holy images painted on wood or tin). Colorful handwoven Hispanic textiles, tinwork, ironwork, and straw appliqué are also in demand. Native American textiles, rugs, katsina dolls, baskets, silver jewelry, turquoise, pottery, beadwork, ornamental shields, drums, and ceramics can be found almost everywhere. Prices range from thousands of dollars for a rare 1930s katsina doll to a few cents for hand-wrapped bundles of sage, juniper, sweet grass, and lavender that are used by Native Americans in healing ceremonies, gatherings, and daily cleansing of the home.

Spices

Roadside stands sell chile ristras, and shops all over the state carry chile powder and other spices. You'll catch the smell of chile peppers from the road; walk in a store and your eyes may water and your mouth salivate. For many, especially natives of the Southwest, *picante* is the purest, finest word in the Spanish language. It means hot—spicy hot. All around you, in boxes, bags, packets, jars, and cans, there's everything picante—salsas, chile pastes, powders, herbs, spices, peppers, barbecue sauce, and fiery potions in bottles.

In This Chapter

Updated by Andrew Collins

santa fe

WITH ITS CRISP, CLEAR AIR and bright, sunny weather, Santa Fe couldn't be more welcoming. On a plateau at the base of the Sangre de Cristo Mountains—at an elevation of 7,000 ft—the city is surrounded by remnants of a 2,000-year-old Pueblo civilization and filled with reminders of almost four centuries of Spanish and Mexican rule. The town's placid central Plaza, which dates from the early 17th century, has been the site of bullfights, public floggings, gunfights, battles, political rallies, promenades, and public markets over the years. A one-of-a-kind destination, Santa Fe is fabled for its rows of chic art galleries, superb restaurants, and shops selling southwestern furnishings and cowboy gear.

La Villa Real de la Santa Fe de San Francisco de Asís (the Royal City of the Holy Faith of St. Francis of Assisi) was founded in the early 1600s by Don Pedro de Peralta, who planted his banner in the name of Spain. In 1680 the region's Pueblo people rose in revolt, burning homes and churches and killing hundreds of Spaniards. After an extended siege in Santa Fe, the Spanish colonists were driven out of New Mexico. The tide turned 12 years later, when General Don Diego de Vargas returned with a new army from El Paso and recaptured Santa Fe.

To commemorate de Vargas's victory, Las Fiestas de Santa Fe have been held every year since 1712. The nation's oldest community celebration takes place on the weekend after Labor Day, with parades, mariachi bands, pageants, the burning of Zozóbra—also known as Old Man Gloom—and nonstop parties. "Fiesta" (as it's referred to locally) is but one of many annual opportunities for revelry—from the arrival of the rodeo and the opening week of the Santa Fe Opera in summer to traditional Pueblo dances at Christmastime.

Following de Vargas's defeat of the Pueblos, the then-grand Camino Real (Royal Road), stretching from Mexico City to Santa Fe, brought an army of conquistadors, clergymen, and settlers to the northernmost reaches of Spain's New World conquests. In 1820 the Santa Fe Trail—a prime artery of U.S. westward expansion—spilled a flood of covered wagons from Missouri onto the Plaza. A booming trade with the United States was born. After Mexico achieved independence from Spain in 1821, its subsequent rule of New Mexico further increased this commerce.

The Santa Fe Trail's heyday ended with the arrival of the Atchison, Topeka & Santa Fe Railway in 1880. The trains, and later the nation's first highways, brought a new type of settler to Santa Fe—artists who fell in love with its cultural diversity, history, and magical color and light. Their presence attracted tourists, who quickly became a primary source of income for the largely poor populace.

Santa Fe is renowned for its arts, tricultural (Native American, Hispanic, and Anglo) heritage, and adobe architecture. The Pueblo people introduced adobe to the Spanish, who in turn developed the adobe brick style of construction. In a relatively dry, treeless region, adobe was a suitable natural building material. Melding into the landscape with their earthen colors and rounded, flowing lines, the pueblos and villages were hard to see from afar and thus somewhat camouflaged from raiding nomadic tribes. The region's distinctive architecture no longer repels visitors, it attracts them.

Among the smallest state capitals in the country, Santa Fe has no major airport (Albuquerque's is the nearest). The city's population, an estimated 62,000, swells to nearly double that figure in summer. In winter the skiers arrive, lured by the challenging slopes of Ski Santa Fe and Taos Ski Valley. Geared for tourists, Santa Fe can put a serious dent in your travel budget. Prices are highest June–August. Between September and November and between April and May they're lower, and (except for the major holidays) from December to March they're the lowest.

HERE AND THERE

Humorist Will Rogers said on his first visit to Santa Fe, "Whoever designed this town did so while riding on a jackass, backwards, and drunk." The maze of narrow streets and alleyways confounds motorists, but with shops and restaurants, a flowered courtyard, or an eye-catching gallery at nearly every turn they're a delight for pedestrians. The trickle of water called the Santa Fe River runs west, parallel to Alameda Street, from the Sangre de Cristo Mountains to the open prairie southwest of town, where it disappears into a narrow canyon before joining the Rio Grande. But in New Mexico there is a *dicho*, or old saying, "*agua es vida*"— "water is life"—be it ever so humble.

There are five state museums in Santa Fe, and purchasing a Museum of New Mexico pass is this most economical way to visit them all. The four-day pass costs $15 and is sold at all five of the museums, which include the Palace of the Governors, Museum of Fine Arts, Museum of Indian Arts and Culture, Museum of International Folk Art, and Museum of Spanish Colonial Art.

SANTA FE PLAZA

Much of the history of Santa Fe, New Mexico, the Southwest, and even the West has some association with Santa Fe's central Plaza, which New Mexico governor Don Pedro de Peralta laid out in 1607. The Plaza, already well established by the time of the Pueblo revolt in 1680, was the site of a bullring and of fiestas and fandangos. Freight wagons unloaded here after completing

santa fe

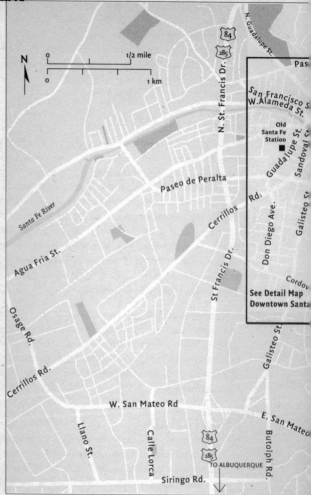

N

0   1/2 mile

0   1 km

N. Guadalupe St.

84
285

Pas

San Francisco S
W. Alameda St.

Old
Santa Fe
Station

Guadalupe St.

Sandoval St

N. St. Francis Dr.

Paseo de Peralta

Santa Fe River

Cerrillos   Rd.

Don Diego Ave.

Galisteo St

Agua Fria St.

St Francis Dr.

Cordov

See Detail Map
Downtown Santa

Osage Rd.

Galisteo St.

Cerrillos Rd.

W. San Mateo Rd

E. San Mateo

Llano St.

Calle Lorca

84
285
TO ALBUQUERQUE

Butolph Rd.

Siringo Rd.

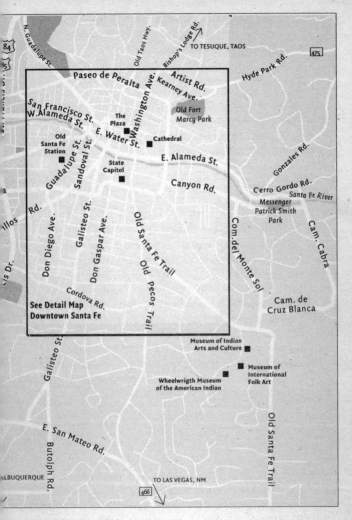

84

N. Guadalupe St.

Old Taos Hwy.

Bishop's Lodge Rd.

TO TESUQUE, TAOS

Hyde Park Rd.

475

Paseo de Peralta

Artist Rd.

Washington Ave.

Kearney Ave.

San Francisco St.

W. Alameda St.

The Plaza

E. Water St.

Cathedral

Old Fort Marcy Park

Gonzales Rd.

Old Santa Fe Station

Guadalupe St.

Sandoval St.

E. Alameda St.

State Capitol

Canyon Rd.

Cerro Gordo Rd.

Santa Fe River

Messenger Patrick Smith Park

Cam. Cabra

Rd.

llos

s Dr.

Don Diego Ave.

Galisteo St.

Don Gaspar Ave.

Old Santa Fe Trail

Old Pecos Trail

Com. del Monte Sol

Cam. de Cruz Blanca

Cordova Rd.

See Detail Map Downtown Santa Fe

Museum of Indian Arts and Culture

Galisteo St.

Wheelwright Museum of the American Indian

Museum of International Folk Art

Old Santa Fe Trail

E. San Mateo Rd.

Butolph Rd.

LBUQUERQUE

TO LAS VEGAS, NM

466

their arduous journey across the Santa Fe Trail. The American flag was raised over the Plaza in 1846, during the Mexican War, which resulted in Mexico's loss of all its territories in the present southwestern United States. For a time the Plaza was a tree-shaded park with a white picket fence. In the 1890s it was an expanse of lawn where uniformed bands played in an ornate gazebo. Particularly festive times on the Plaza are the weekend after Labor Day, during Las Fiestas de Santa Fe, and at Christmas, when all the trees are filled with lights and rooftops are outlined with *farolitos*, votive candles lit within paper-bag lanterns.

Numbers in the text correspond to numbers in the margin and on the Downtown Santa Fe map.

What to See

❸ **GEORGIA O'KEEFFE MUSEUM.** One of many East Coast artists who visited New Mexico in the first half of the 20th century, O'Keeffe fell in love with the region and returned to live and paint here, eventually emerging as the demigoddess of southwestern art. This private museum devoted to the works of this Modernist painter opened in 1997. O'Keeffe's innovative view of the landscape is captured in *From the Plains*, inspired by her memory of the Texas plains, and *Jimson Weed*, a quintessential O'Keeffe study of one of her favorite plants. Special exhibitions with O'Keeffe's Modernist peers are on view throughout the year. Unfortunately, the museum provides relatively little context for O'Keeffe's works or biographical information about her life. *217 Johnson St., tel. 505/995–0785, www.okeeffemuseum.org. $5, free Fri. 5–8 PM. July–Oct., Sat.–Thurs. 10–5, Fri. 10–8; Nov.–June, Thurs. and Sat.–Tues. 10–5, Fri. 10–8.*

❻ **INSTITUTE OF AMERICAN INDIAN ARTS MUSEUM.** Inside the handsomely renovated former post office, this museum contains the largest collection of contemporary Native American art in the United States. The paintings, photography, sculptures, prints, and traditional crafts exhibited here were created by past and present

downtown santa fe

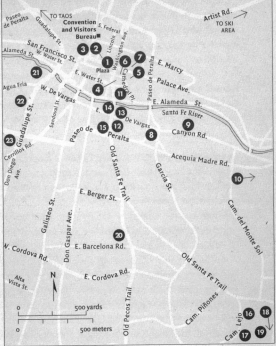

Barrio de
Analco, **14**

Cristo Rey
Church, **10**

El Zaguan, **9**

Georgia O'Keeffe
Museum, **3**

Gerald Peters
Gallery, **8**

Institute of
American Indian
Arts Musum, **6**

La Fonda, **4**

Loretto
Chapel, **11**

Museum of
Fine Arts, **2**

Museum of
Indian Arts and
Culture, **16**

Museum of
International
Folk Art, **17**

Museum of
Spanish Colonial
Art, **18**

New Mexico State
Capitol, **15**

The Oldest
House, **13**

Palace of the
Governors, **1**

Saint Francis
Cathedral, **5**

San Miguel
Mission, **12**

Santa Fe Children's
Museum, **20**

Santa Fe Southern
Railway, **22**

Santuario de
Guadalupe, **21**

Sena Plaza, **7**

SITE Santa Fe, **23**

Wheelwright
Museum of the
American
Indian, **19**

students and teachers. The institute itself, which moved to the College of Santa Fe campus, was founded as a one-room studio classroom in the early 1930s by Dorothy Dunn, a beloved art teacher who played a critical role in launching the careers of many Native American artists. In the 1960s and 1970s it blossomed into the nation's premier center for Native American arts. Artist Fritz Scholder taught here for years, as did the sculptor Allan Houser. Among their disciples was the painter T. C. Cannon. *108 Cathedral Pl., tel. 505/983–8900; 505/983–1777 information line; www.iaiancad.org/museum.htm. $4. June–Sept., Mon.–Sat. 9–5, Sun. 10–5; Oct.–May, Mon.–Sat. 10–5, Sun. noon–5.*

4 **LA FONDA.** A Santa Fe landmark, La Fonda faces the southeast corner of the Plaza. A *fonda* (inn) has stood on this site for centuries. Architect Isaac Hamilton Rapp, whose Rio Grande–Pueblo Revival structures put Santa Fe style on the map, built this hotel in 1922. The hotel was remodeled in 1926 by another luminary of Santa Fe architecture, John Gaw Meem. The hotel was sold to the Santa Fe Railway in 1926 and became one of Fred Harvey's Harvey House hotels until 1968. Because of its proximity to the Plaza and its history as a gathering place for cowboys, trappers, traders, soldiers, frontier politicians, movie stars (Errol Flynn stayed here), artists, and writers, it is referred to as "the Inn at the End of the Trail." Major social events still take place here. A great way to experience the hotel is with a drink at the fifth-floor Bell Tower Bar (open late spring–early fall), which offers tremendous sunset views. *E. San Francisco St. at Old Santa Fe Trail, tel. 505/982–5511.*

NEED A BREAK? **CARLOS' GOSP'L CAFE** (125 Lincoln Ave., tel. 505/983–1841) has a black-and-white checked floor and some patio chairs; it's hidden in a courtyard behind the Palace of the Governors and serves just about the best pies in town, always baked fresh daily. Great sandwiches are served, too. The gorgeous space of the **LONGEVITY CAFÉ & EMPORIUM** (Plaza Mercado center, 2nd floor, Water and Galisteo Sts., tel. 505/986–0403), with a latilla-

and-viga ceiling, leather sofas, and cool music, draws a quirky crowd and is open late. Have a cup of organic tea and a homemade dessert like pumpkin pie with ginseng-chai, or pick up holistic books and East Asian tea ware.

★ ❷ **MUSEUM OF FINE ARTS.** Designed by Isaac Hamilton Rapp in 1917, the museum contains one of America's finest regional collections. It's also one of Santa Fe's earliest Pueblo Revival structures, inspired by the adobe structures at Acoma Pueblo. Split-cedar *latillas* (branches set in a crosshatch pattern) and hand-hewn vigas form the ceilings. The 8,000-piece permanent collection, of which only a fraction is exhibited at any given time, emphasizes the work of regional and nationally renowned artists, including the early Modernist Georgia O'Keeffe; realist Robert Henri; the "Cinco Pintores" (five painters) of Santa Fe (including Fremont Elis and Will Shuster); members of the Taos Society of Artists (Ernest L. Blumenschein, Bert G. Philips, Joseph H. Sharp, and E. Irving Couse, among others); and the works of noted 20th-century photographers of the Southwest, including Laura Gilpin, Ansel Adams, and Dorothea Lange. Many excellent examples of Spanish colonial–style furniture are on display. An interior *placita* (small plaza) with fountains, WPA murals, and sculpture and the St. Francis Auditorium are other highlights. *107 W. Palace Ave., tel. 505/476–5072, www.nmculture.org. $7, 4-day pass $15 (good at all 5 state museums in Santa Fe), free Fri. 5–8 PM. Tues.–Thurs. and weekends 10–5, Fri. 10–8.*

★ ☙ ❶ **PALACE OF THE GOVERNORS.** A humble-looking one-story adobe on the north side of the Plaza, the palace is the oldest public building in the United States. Built at the same time as the Plaza, circa 1610 (scholars debate the exact year), it was the seat of four regional governments—those of Spain, Mexico, the Confederacy, and the U.S. territory that preceded New Mexico's statehood, which was achieved in 1912. It served as the residence for 100 Spanish, Mexican, and American governors, including Governor Lew Wallace, who wrote his epic *Ben Hur* in its then drafty rooms, all the while complaining of the dust and mud that fell from its earthen ceiling. In 2003, construction is scheduled to begin on a brand-new State History Museum, which will stand directly behind the Palace and is expected to open in 2005. Simultaneously, the Palace of the Governors is slated to be renovated to a house-museum. Its rooms will contain period furnishings and exhibits that illustrate the building's myriad functions over the past four centuries.

Dozens of Native American vendors gather daily under the portal of the Palace of the Governors to display and sell pottery, jewelry, bread, and other goods. With few exceptions, the more than 500 artists and craftspeople registered to sell here are Pueblo or Navajo Indians. The merchandise for sale is required to meet Museum of New Mexico standards: all items are handmade or hand-strung in Native American households; silver jewelry is either sterling (92.5% pure) or coin (90% pure) silver; all metal jewelry bears the maker's mark, which is registered with the museum. Prices tend to reflect the high quality of the merchandise. Don't take photographs without permission.

The palace has been the central headquarters of the Museum of New Mexico since 1913, housing the main section of the **State History Museum.** Permanent exhibits chronicle 450 years of New Mexico history, using maps, furniture, clothing, housewares, weaponry, and village models. With advance permission, students and researchers have access to the comprehensive **Fray Angélico Chávez Library** and its rare maps, manuscripts, and photographs (more than 120,000 prints and negatives). The palace is also home to the **Museum of New Mexico Press,** which prints books, pamphlets, and cards on antique presses and hosts bookbinding demonstrations, lectures, and slide shows. There is an outstanding gift shop and bookstore. *Palace Ave., north side of the Plaza, tel. 505/476–5100, www.palaceofthegovernors.org. $7, 4-day pass $15 (good at all 5 state* museums in Santa Fe), free Fri. 5–8. Tues.–Thurs. and weekends 10–5, Fri. 10–8.

★ ⑤ **ST. FRANCIS CATHEDRAL.** This magnificent cathedral, a block east of the Plaza, is one of the rare significant departures from the city's ubiquitous Pueblo architecture. Construction was begun in 1869 by Jean Baptiste Lamy, Santa Fe's first archbishop, working with French architects and Italian stonemasons. The Romanesque style was popular in Lamy's native home in the southwest of France. The circuit-riding cleric was sent by the Catholic Church to the Southwest to change the religious practices of its native population (to "civilize" them, as one period document puts it) and is buried in the crypt beneath the church's high altar. He was the inspiration behind Willa Cather's novel *Death Comes for the Archbishop* (1927).

A small adobe chapel on the northeast side of the cathedral, the remnant of an earlier church, embodies the Hispanic architectural influence so conspicuously absent from the cathedral itself. The chapel's *Nuestra Señora de la Paz* (Our Lady of Peace), popularly known as *La Conquistadora*, the oldest Madonna statue in the United States, accompanied Don Diego de Vargas on his reconquest of Santa Fe in 1692, a feat attributed to the statue's spiritual intervention. Every Friday the faithful adorn the statue with a new dress. Just south of the cathedral, where the parking lot meets Paseo de Peralta, is the **Archives of the Archdiocese Museum** (tel. 505/983–3811), a small museum where many of the area's historic, liturgical artifacts are on view. *231 Cathedral Pl., tel. 505/982–5619. Daily 8–5:45, except during mass. Mass Mon.–Sat. at 7 and 8:15 AM, 12:10, and 5:15 PM; Sun. at 6, 8, and 10 AM, noon, and 7 PM. Museum weekdays 9–noon and 1–4.*

⑦ **SENA PLAZA.** Two-story buildings enclose this courtyard, which can be entered only through two small doorways on Palace Avenue. Surrounding the oasis of flowering fruit trees, a fountain, and inviting benches are unique, low-profile shops. The quiet courtyard is a good place for repose. The buildings, erected in the 1700s as a single-family residence, had quarters for blacksmiths, bakers, farmers, and all manner of help. *125 E. Palace Ave.*

CANYON ROAD

Once a Native American trail and an early 20th-century route for woodcutters and their burros, Canyon Road is now lined with art galleries, shops, and restaurants, earning it the nickname "the Art and Soul of Santa Fe." The narrow road begins at the eastern curve of Paseo de Peralta and stretches for about 2 mi at a moderate incline toward the base of the mountains.

Most establishments are in authentic, old adobe homes with undulating thick walls that appear to have been carved out of the earth. Within many are contemporary and traditional works by artists with internationally renowned names like Fernando Botero to anonymous weavers of ancient Peruvian textiles.

There are few places as festive as Canyon Road on Christmas Eve, when thousands of farolitos illuminate walkways, walls, roofs, and even trees. In May, the scent of lilacs wafts over the adobe walls, and in August red hollyhocks enhance the surreal color of the blue sky on a dry summer day.

What to See

⑩ **CRISTO REY CHURCH.** Built in 1940 to commemorate the 400th anniversary of Francisco Vásquez de Coronado's exploration of the Southwest, this church is the largest Spanish adobe structure in the United States and is considered by many the finest example of Pueblo-style architecture anywhere. The church was constructed in the old-fashioned way by parishioners, who mixed the more than 200,000 mud-and-straw adobe bricks and hauled them into place. The 225-ton stone reredos (altar screen) is magnificent. *Canyon Rd. at Cristo Rey, tel. 505/983–8528. Daily 8–7.*

9 **EL ZAGUAN.** Headquarters of the **Historic Santa Fe Foundations (HSFF),** this 19th-century Territorial-style house has a small exhibit on Santa Fe architecture and preservation, but the real draw is the small but stunning garden abundant with lavender, roses, and 160-year-old trees. You can relax on a wrought-iron bench and take in the fine views of the hills northeast of town. An HSFF horticulturist often gives free tours and lectures in the garden on Thursdays at 1 in summer (call to confirm). *545 Canyon Rd., tel. 505/983–2567, www.historicsantafe.com. Free. Foundations offices weekdays 9–noon and 1:30–5; gardens Mon.–Sat. 9–5.*

8 **GERALD PETERS GALLERY.** While under construction, this 32,000-square-ft building was dubbed the "ninth northern pueblo," its scale rivaling that of the eight northern pueblos around Santa Fe. The suavely designed Pueblo-style gallery is Santa Fe's premier showcase for American and European art from the 19th century to the present. It feels like a museum, but all the works are for sale. Pablo Picasso, Georgia O'Keeffe, Charles M. Russell, Deborah Butterfield, George Rickey, and members of the Taos Society are among the artists represented, along with nationally renowned contemporary ones. *1011 Paseo de Peralta, tel. 505/954–5700, www.gpgallery.com. Free. Mon.–Sat. 10–5.*

NEED A BREAK? A good place to rest your feet is the **BACKROOM COFFEEBAR** (616 Canyon Rd., tel. 505/988–5323), which serves pastries and light snacks. Locals congregate in the courtyard or on the front portal of **DOWNTOWN SUBSCRIPTION** (376 Garcia St., tel. 505/983–3085) a block east of Canyon Road. This café-newsstand sells coffees, snacks, and pastries, plus one of the largest assortments of newspapers and magazines in New Mexico.

LOWER OLD SANTA FE TRAIL

It was along the Old Santa Fe Trail that wagon trains from Missouri rolled into town in the 1800s, forever changing Santa Fe's destiny. This area off the Plaza is one of Santa Fe's most historic.

What to See

⑭ **BARRIO DE ANALCO.** Along the south bank of the Santa Fe River, the barrio—its name means "district on the other side of the water"—is one of America's oldest neighborhoods, settled in the early 1600s by the Tlaxcalan Indians (who were forbidden to live with the Spanish near the Plaza) and in the 1690s by soldiers who had helped recapture New Mexico after the Pueblo Revolt. Plaques on houses on East De Vargas Street will help you locate some of the important structures. Check the performance schedule at the **Santa Fe Playhouse** on De Vargas Street, founded by writer Mary Austin and other Santa Feans in the 1920s.

⑪ **LORETTO CHAPEL.** A delicate Gothic church modeled after Sainte-Chapelle in Paris, Loretto was built in 1873 by the same French architects and Italian stonemasons who built St. Francis Cathedral. The chapel is known for the "Miraculous Staircase" that leads to the choir loft. Legend has it that the chapel was almost complete when it became obvious that there wasn't room to build a staircase to the choir loft. In answer to the prayers of the cathedral's nuns, a mysterious carpenter arrived on a donkey, built a 20-ft staircase—using only a square, a saw, and a tub of water to season the wood—and then disappeared as quickly as he came. Many of the faithful believed it was St. Joseph himself. The staircase contains two complete 360-degree turns with no central support; no nails were used in its construction. The chapel closes for services and special events. Adjoining the chapel are a small museum and gift shop. 211 *Old Santa Fe Trail, tel. 505/982-0092, www.lorettochapel.com. $2.50. Mid-Oct.–mid-May, Mon.–Sat. 9–5, Sun. 10:30–5; mid-May–mid-Oct., Mon.–Sat. 9–6, Sun. 10:30–5.*

⑮ **NEW MEXICO STATE CAPITOL.** The symbol of the Zía Pueblo, which represents the Circle of Life, was the inspiration for the Capitol, also known as the Roundhouse. Doorways at opposing sides of this 1966 structure symbolize the four winds, the four directions, and the four seasons. Throughout the building are artworks from the outstanding collection of the Capitol Art

Foundation, historical and cultural displays, and handcrafted furniture. The **Governor's Gallery** hosts temporary exhibits. Six acres of imaginatively landscaped gardens shelter outstanding sculptures. *Old Santa Fe Trail at Paseo de Peralta, tel. 505/986–4589. Free. Mid-May–Aug., Mon.–Sat. 8–7; Sept.–mid-May, weekdays 8–7; tours by appointment.*

⓭ **THE OLDEST HOUSE.** More than 800 years ago, Pueblo people built this structure out of "puddled" adobe (liquid mud poured between upright wooden frames). This house, which contains a gift shop, is said to be the oldest in the United States. *215 E. De Vargas St.*

★ ⓬ **SAN MIGUEL MISSION.** The oldest church still in use in the United States, this simple earth-hue adobe structure was built in the early 17th century by the Tlaxcalan Indians of Mexico, who came to New Mexico as servants of the Spanish. Badly damaged in the 1680 Pueblo Revolt, the structure was restored and enlarged in 1710. On display in the chapel are priceless statues and paintings and the San José Bell, weighing nearly 800 pounds, which is believed to have been cast in Spain in 1356. In winter, the church sometimes closes before its official closing hour. Mass is held on Sunday at 5 PM. Next door in the back of the Territorial-style dormitories of the old St. Michael's High School, a **Visitor Information Center** can help you find your way around northern New Mexico. *401 Old Santa Fe Trail, tel. 505/983–3974. $1. Mission Mon.–Sat. 10–4, Sun. 3–4:30.*

UPPER OLD SANTA FE TRAIL

What to See

★ ⓰ **MUSEUM OF INDIAN ARTS AND CULTURE.** An interactive, multimedia exhibition tells the story of Native American history in the Southwest, merging contemporary Native American experience with historical accounts and artifacts. The collection has some of New Mexico's oldest works of art: pottery vessels, fine stone and silver jewelry, intricate textiles, and other arts and crafts created by Pueblo, Navajo, and Apache artisans. You can also see art demonstrations and a video about the life and work of Pueblo potter Maria Martinez. *710 Camino Lejo, tel. 505/476–1250, www.miaclab.org. $7, 4-day pass $15 (good at all 5 state museums in Santa Fe). Tues.–Sun. 10–5.*

★ ⑰ **MUSEUM OF INTERNATIONAL FOLK ART.** Everywhere you look in this facility, the premier institution of its kind in the world, you'll find amazingly inventive handmade objects—a tin Madonna, a devil made from bread dough, and all kinds of rag dolls. Florence Dibell Bartlett, who founded the museum in 1953, donated its first 4,000 works. In the late 1970s Alexander and Susan Girard, major folk-art collectors, gave the museum 106,000 items. The Hispanic Heritage Wing contains 5,000 pieces (mostly religious works, such as carved wooden statues of saints) dating from the Spanish-colonial period (in New Mexico, 1598–1821) to the present. *706 Camino Lejo, tel. 505/476–1200, www.moifa.org. $7, 4-day pass $15 (good at all 5 state museums in Santa Fe). Tues.–Sun. 10–5.*

⑱ **MUSEUM OF SPANISH COLONIAL ART.** Opened in July 2002, this 5,000-square-ft adobe museum occupies a building designed in 1930 by acclaimed architect John Gaw Meem. The Spanish Colonial Art Society formed in Santa Fe in 1925 to preserve traditional Spanish-colonial art and culture. The museum, which sits next to the Museum of New Mexico complex, displays the fruits of the society's labor—one of the most comprehensive collections of Spanish-colonial art in the world. The Hale Matthews Library contains a 1,000-volume collection of books relating to this important period in art history. Objects here, dating from the 16th century to the present, include retablos, elaborate santos, tinwork, straw appliqué, furniture, ceramics, and ironwork. There's also a fine collection of works by Hispanic artists of the 20th century. *750 Camino Lejo, tel. 505/982–2226, www.spanishcolonial.org/museum.shtml. $6, 4-day pass $15 (good at all 5 state museums in Santa Fe). Daily 10–5.*

☙ ⑳ **SANTA FE CHILDREN'S MUSEUM.** Stimulating hands-on exhibits, a solar greenhouse, oversize geometric forms, and a simulated 18-ft mountain-climbing wall all contribute to the museum's popularity with kids. Puppeteers and storytellers occasionally perform. 1050 *Old Pecos Trail, tel. 505/989–8359, www.santafechildrensmuseum.org.* $3. Sept.–May, Thurs.–Sat. 10–5, Sun. noon–5; June–Aug., Wed.–Sat. 10–5, Sun. noon–5.

⑲ **WHEELWRIGHT MUSEUM OF THE AMERICAN INDIAN.** A private institution in a building shaped like a traditional octagonal Navajo hogan, the Wheelwright opened in 1937. Founded by Boston scholar Mary Cabot Wheelwright and Navajo medicine man Hastiin Klah, the museum originated as a place to house ceremonial materials. Those items are not on view to the public. What is displayed are 19th- and 20th-century baskets, pottery, sculpture, weavings, metalwork, photography, and paintings, including contemporary works by Native American artists. The Case Trading Post on the lower level is modeled after the trading posts that dotted the southwestern frontier more than 100 years ago. It carries an extensive selection of books and contemporary Native American jewelry, katsina dolls, weaving, and pottery. *704 Camino Lejo, tel. 505/982–4636 or 800/607–4636, www.wheelwright.org. Free. Mon.–Sat. 10–5, Sun. 1–5; gallery tours Mon.–Tues. and Fri. at 2, Sat. at 11.*

HISTORIC GUADALUPE RAILROAD DISTRICT

The historic warehouse district of Santa Fe is commonly referred to as the Railyard or Guadalupe District. After the demise of the train route through town, the low-lying warehouses were converted to artist studios and antiques shops, and bookstores, specialty shops, and restaurants have sprung up. The restored scenic train line puts the town's old depot to use. The local farmers' market turns the depot parking lot into a colorful outdoor fiesta.

What to See

㉒ SANTA FE SOUTHERN RAILWAY. For a leisurely tour across the Santa Fe plateau and into the vast Galisteo Basin, where panoramic views extend for up to 120 mi, take a nostalgic ride on the antique cars of the Santa Fe Southern Railway. The train once served a spur of the Atchison, Topeka & Santa Fe Railway. Today the train takes visitors on 36-mi round-trip scenic trips to Lamy, a sleepy village with the region's only Amtrak service, offering picnics under the cottonwoods (bring your own or buy one from the caterer that meets the train) at the quaint rail station. Aside from day trips, the railway offers special events such as a Friday-night "High Desert High Ball" cash bar with appetizers and a "Sunset Run," on which a barbecue, a campfire, and live entertainment await you at the Lamy depot. Trains depart from the Santa Fe Depot, rebuilt in 1909 after the original was destroyed in a fire. There's talk of eventually opening a regional transportation and rail museum here. *410 S. Guadalupe St., tel. 505/989–8600 or 888/989–8600, www.sfsr.com. Reservations essential. Day trips from $25, "Sunset Run" from $45, High Desert High Ball from $40. Call for schedule.*

㉑ SANTUARIO DE GUADALUPE. A humble adobe structure built by Franciscan missionaries between 1776 and 1795, this is the oldest shrine in the United States to Our Lady of Guadalupe, patron saint of Mexico. The sanctuary, now a nonprofit cultural center, has adobe walls nearly 3 ft thick. Among the sanctuary's religious art and artifacts is a priceless 16th-century work by Venetian painter Leonardo de Ponte Bassano that depicts Jesus driving the money changers from the Temple. Also of note is a portrait of Our Lady of Guadalupe by the Mexican colonial painter José de Alzíbar. Other highlights are the traditional New Mexican carved and painted altar screen, an authentic 19th-century sacristy, a pictorial-history archive, a library devoted to Archbishop Jean Baptiste Lamy that is furnished with many of his belongings, and a garden with plants from the Holy Land. *100 Guadalupe St., tel. 505/988–2027. Donation suggested. Mon.–Sat. 9–4.*

SITE SANTA FE. The events at this nexus of international contemporary art include lectures, concerts, author readings, performance art, and gallery shows. The facility hosts a biennial exhibition every odd-numbered year. There are always provocative exhibitions here, however, and the immense, open space is ideal for taking in the many larger-than-life installations. *1606 Paseo de Peralta, tel. 505/989–1199, www.sitesantafe.org. $5, free Fri. Wed.– Thurs. and weekends 10–5, Fri. 10–7.*

EATING OUT

So-called Santa Fe–style cuisine has so many influences that the term is virtually meaningless. Traditional, old-style Santa Fe restaurants serve New Mexican fare, which combines both Native American and Hispanic traditions and differs markedly from most Americanized Mexican cooking. Many of the better restaurants in town serve a contemporary regional style of cooking that blends New Mexican ingredients and preparations with those of interior and coastal Mexico, Latin America, the Mediterranean, East Asian, and varied parts of the United States. There are several high-caliber Italian restaurants in town, and a growing number of commendable Asian eateries, but all in all the city's culinary diversity is limited.

AMERICAN/CASUAL

$–$$ BOBCAT BITE. This divey grill in a tiny house a 15-minute drive south of town serves steaks and chops but is famous for one thing: the biggest and juiciest burgers in town. Locals prefer them topped with cheese and green chiles. The hours vary and can be a bit limited, so call ahead. *Old Las Vegas Hwy., 4½ mi south of the Old Pecos Trail exit off I–25, tel. 505/983–5319. Reservations not accepted. No credit cards.*

$–$$ COWGIRL HALL OF FAME. A rollicking and fanatically popular bar and grill with several atmospheric rooms overflowing with Old West

downtown santa fe dining

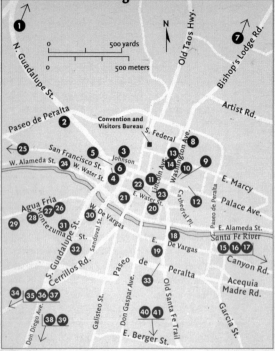

memorabilia, Cowgirl deserves kudos for its reasonably priced and nearly always quite tasty southwestern, Tex-Mex, barbecue, and southern fare. Highlights include sizzling barbecue, bourbon-glazed pork chops, and salmon tacos with a kicky tomatillo salsa. So what's the drawback? Consistently subpar service. Nevertheless, knock back a few drinks and catch one of the nightly music acts—usually rock or blues—and you're likely to leave smiling. Grab a seat on the spacious patio in warm weather. 319 S. Guadalupe St., tel. 505/982-2565. AE, D, MC, V.

$–$$ ZIA DINER. This slick diner with a low-key, art deco–style interior serves comfort food prepared with the occasional nouvelle twist. Stop in for a full meal (ask about the night's blue-plate special, like Friday's fish Vera Cruz style) or just a thick slice of fresh strawberry-rhubarb pie. Service is fast and friendly, and the food is fresh. There's a cheerful patio. 326 S. Guadalupe St., tel. 505/988-7008. AE, MC, V.

$ ATOMIC GRILL. Burgers, salads, pizzas, sandwiches, and other light munchies are served at this tiny late-night café a block off the Plaza. The food is decent and the service brusque but usually okay. The best attributes are the comfy patio overlooking pedestrian-heavy Water Street, the huge list of imported beers, and the late hours (it's open til 3 most nights)—an extreme rarity in Santa Fe. You'll be glad this place exists when the bars let out and you're famished. 103 Water St., tel. 505/820-2866. MC, V.

$ TESUQUE VILLAGE MARKET. ★ A favorite spot for a snack or a full meal before heading to the opera or after a shopping at the Tesuque Pueblo Flea Market, this epicurean grocery and people-watching café has a tiny but lovely patio and a less atmospheric indoor seating area. The kitchen serves up tasty American and New Mexican fare—pork chops verde, *posole* stew (soup made with lime hominy, pork, chile, and garlic), French toast, Frito pie. Save room for a fresh-baked brownie or cookie. NM 599 at Bishop's Lodge Rd., Tesuque, 5 mi north of Santa Fe, tel. 505/988-8848. Reservations not accepted. MC, V.

CAFÉS

$–$$ O'KEEFFE CAFE. This swanky café at the Georgia O'Keeffe Museum turns out some of the best lunch fare in Santa Fe. The spinach-chèvre salad with jícama, avocado, pine nuts, and a sage vinaigrette scores high marks, as does an entrée of seared salmon with a cilantro-lime dressing served over mashed potatoes with an ancho-chile mole. The management also operates the Museum Hill Cafe at Milner Plaza, outside the folk and Indian art museums. *217 Johnson St., tel. 505/992–1065. AE, MC, V. Closed Sun.–Mon. No dinner.*

$ SANTA FE BAKING COMPANY. Breakfast tends to be a big social affair in Santa Fe, and several very good bakeries vie heavily for the morning crowd. Although it's located at a strip shopping center just south of town, Santa Fe Baking prepares some of the best food—massive breakfast burritos, fluffy French toast, and blue-corn pancakes. At lunch, it's great for copious deli sandwiches. Order at the counter and grab a seat in the high-ceilinged, light-filled dining room. *504 W. Cordova Rd., tel. 505/988–4292. Reservations not accepted. AE, MC, V. No dinner.*

CONTEMPORARY

$$$$ ANASAZI RESTAURANT. Soft light illuminates the Chaco Canyon–inspired sandstone walls and adobe interior of this restaurant, which became a Santa Fe fixture the day it opened. The kitchen combines New Mexican and Native American ingredients to produce such exotic fare as buffalo carpaccio with parsley-sage oil and blackberry–whole grain mustard as well as blue corn–dusted diver scallops with chile-dipped shrimp, corn puree, and blood-orange coulis. The large dining room has wooden tables and *bancos* (benches built into the plastered walls) upholstered with handwoven textiles from Chimayó. The Sunday brunch is excellent. *113 Washington Ave., tel. 505/988–3236. AE, D, DC, MC, V.*

$$$$ THE COMPOUND. Three decades ago, this handsome adobe
★ tucked down an alley off Canyon Road epitomized white-glove

fine dining. Its fortunes waxed and waned over the years before acclaimed restaurateurs Brett Kemmerer and Mark Kiffin rescued it from oblivion and transformed it into one of the state's culinary darlings. It's still a fancy place, but dress is a cut below formal, and the staff highly attentive but also easy-going. From the oft-changing menu consider a starter of cockle risotto with peas, parsley, reggiano parmigiano, and chorizo broth. Memorable entrées include "forever-braised" bone-in pork leg with mustard greens, roasted apples, small turnips, and fresh horseradish; or buttermilk roast chicken with creamed fresh spinach and foie gras pan gravy. *653 Canyon Rd., tel. 505/982–4353. AE, D, DC, MC, V. No lunch weekends.*

\$\$\$\$ **COYOTE CAFE AND ROOFTOP CANTINA.** Touristy, bold, and presided over by celebrity chef Mark Miller, this is the restaurant lots of people love to bad-mouth. Say what you will, Coyote Cafe manages to produce superbly original Southwest cooking, and the service is surprisingly pleasant considering the high expectations and sometimes overwhelming crowds. Try wild-boar tamale with *huitlacoche* (a type of mushroom) sauce, or the fillet of tea-smoked salmon slow-roasted with fennel and star anise. The open dining room can be loud and obnoxiously showy. On the wine list are more than 500 vintages. Inventive, delicious, mostly under-\$10 fare is served on the open-air Rooftop Cantina April through October—it's highly underrated and is an excellent lunch option. *132 W. Water St., tel. 505/983–1615. Reservations essential. AE, D, DC, MC, V.*

\$\$\$\$ **GERONIMO.** Chef Eric DiStefano changes the menu frequently at
★ this restaurant in the Borrego House, which dates from 1756. A typical meal might start with an appetizer of cold-water lobster tail on angel hair pasta. Entrées are artful, like mesquite-grilled elk tenderloin with smoked bacon and chestnut strudel, or red-corn relleno with duck and black-bean sauce. The Sunday brunch is also impressive. The intimate, white dining rooms have beamed ceilings, wood floors, fireplaces, and cushioned bancos. In summer you can

dine under the front portal; in winter the bar with fireplace is inviting. *724 Canyon Rd., tel. 505/982–1500. AE, MC, V. No lunch Mon.*

$$$–$$$$ CAFE PASQUAL'S. This cheerful cubbyhole dishes up southwestern
★ and Nuevo Latino specialties for breakfast, lunch, and dinner. Don't be discouraged by lines out in front—it's worth the wait. The culinary muse behind it all is Katharine Kagel, who for more than 20 years has been introducing specialties like buttermilk biscuits with sage-bacon gravy, homemade sausage, and poached eggs to diners. Dinner is a more formal affair: the free-range chicken mole enchilada with plantain rice, fresh corn torte, and mango-jícama salad is a pleasure; the kicky starter of spicy Vietnamese squid salad with tamarind, garlic, and lime over baby spinach is also fantastic. Mexican folk art and colorful tiles and murals by Oaxacan artist Leo Vigildo Martinez create a festive atmosphere. Try the communal table if you want to be seated in a hurry. *121 Don Gaspar Ave., tel. 505/983–9340. AE, MC, V.*

$$$–$$$$ OLD HOUSE. Chef Martín Rios changes the menu every Thursday at his fashionably casual restaurant inside the equally fashionable Eldorado Hotel. Entrées have included lavender-honey-glazed Muscovy duck breast and leg confit with creamy white polenta, baby carrots, and natural dark jus. More than two dozen of the impressive wines are served by the glass. A separate dining room has a slightly more refined interior than the hotel-hacienda ambience of the main dining room. *Eldorado Hotel, 309 W. San Francisco St., tel. 505/988–4455. AE, D, DC, MC, V. No lunch.*

$$$–$$$$ RISTRA. This unprepossessing restaurant in the up-and-coming Guadalupe District presents a first-rate menu of southwestern-influenced country French cooking. You might start with a lobster brioche tartlette layered with tomatoes, leeks, caviar, and a lobster sauce; achiote elk tenderloin with morel barley, glazed shallots, baby gold beets, and red wine sauce is a tempting main dish. The wines are well selected and the service is swift and courteous. Navajo blankets hang on stark white walls, and Pueblo pottery adorns the handful of niches. *548 Agua Fria St., tel. 505/982–8608. AE, MC, V. No lunch.*

$$$–$$$$ SANTACAFÉ. Minimalist elegance marks the interior of Santacafé,
★ one of Santa Fe's vanguard "food as art" restaurants, two blocks north of the Plaza in the historic Padre Gallegos House. Seasonal ingredients are included in the inventive dishes, which might include serrano-wrapped cod with white beans, sun-dried tomatoes, and grilled sweet peppers. Poblano chowder makes a terrific starter, as does the sublime crispy-fried calamari with a snappy lime dipping sauce. The patio is a joy in summer, and the bar makes a snazzy spot to meet friends for drinks just about any time of year. If you're on a tight budget, consider the reasonably priced lunch menu. *231 Washington Ave., tel. 505/984–1788. AE, MC, V.*

$$–$$$ PAUL'S. Whimsical painted Oaxacan figurines line a few shelves
★ of this otherwise simple storefront café with a small but well-trained staff. The pumpkin bread stuffed with pine nuts, corn, and green chiles with queso blanco, red-chile sauce, and caramelized apples is a classic specialty, but don't overlook baked salmon with a pecan-herb crust and sorrel sauce. The blue-crab cakes with a tomato-orange-chipotle sauce star among the starters. *72 W. Marcy St., tel. 505/982–8738. AE, D, DC, MC, V. Closed Mon.*

CONTINENTAL

$$$$ LA CASA SENA. The southwestern-accented and Continental fare served at La Casa Sena is rich and beautifully presented. Weather permitting, get a table on the patio surrounded by hollyhocks, flowering shrubs, and centuries-old adobe walls. If you order the *trucha en terra-cotta* (fresh trout wrapped in corn husks and baked in clay), ask your waiter to save the clay head for you as a souvenir. Finish dinner with the wonderful citrus mascarpone tart with orange sauce and Grand Marnier–soaked berries. Weekend brunch dishes are equally elegant. For a musical meal (evenings only), sit in the restaurant's adjacent Cantina, where the talented staff belt out Broadway show tunes. Meals in the Cantina are less expensive, and less exciting. Reservations are essential in summer. *Sena Plaza, 125 E. Palace Ave., tel. 505/988–9232. AE, D, DC, MC, V.*

ECLECTIC

$$–$$$ CAFE SAN ESTEVAN. This place is perfect when you're seeking a restaurant with exceptional New Mexican and Continental fare, all of it prepared simply but with ultrafresh ingredients and superb presentation. The small and rather noisy dining room is charming nonetheless, with some tables facing a corner fireplace. The chiles rellenos here are exceptional, stuffed with cheese and onions and served with rice and *calabacitas* (a kind of squash)— nothing here is greasy or overwrought. Also top-notch are the spaghettini with chicken, cream sauce, and fresh peas. Chef-owner Estevan Garcia puts on a great show. *428 Agua Fria St., tel. 505/995–1996. AE, D, MC, V. Closed Mon.*

$$–$$$ PINK ADOBE. Rosalea Murphy opened her restaurant back in 1944, and the place still seems to reflect a time when fewer than 20,000 people lived in town. The intimate, rambling rooms of this late-17th-century house have fireplaces and artwork and are filled with conversation made over special-occasion meals. The ambience of the restaurant, rather than the food, accounts for its popularity. The steak Dunigan, smothered in green chile and mushrooms, and the savory shrimp Louisianne—fat and deep-fried crispy—are among the Continental, New Orleans creole, and New Mexican dishes served. The apple pie drenched in rum sauce is a favorite. Particularly strong margaritas are mixed in the adjacent Dragon Room bar. *406 Old Santa Fe Trail, tel. 505/983–7712. AE, D, DC, MC, V. No lunch weekends.*

$–$$ HARRY'S ROADHOUSE. This quirky, always-packed adobe
★ compound consists of several inviting rooms, from a diner-style space with counter seating to a cozier nook with a fireplace— there's also an enchanting courtyard out back with juniper trees and flower gardens. The varied menu of contemporary diner favorites, pizzas, New Mexican fare, and bountiful salads is

supplemented by a long list of daily specials. Favorites include Moroccan vegetable stew over couscous with harissa, and grilled-fish tacos with tomatillo salsa and black beans. Breakfast is a favorite meal here—try the blueberry buckwheat pancakes. *Old Las Vegas Hwy., 1 mi south of the Old Pecos Trail exit off I–25, tel. 505/989–4629. AE, D, MC, V.*

$–$$ **PLAZA RESTAURANT.** Run with homespun care by the Razatos
★ family since 1947, this café has been a fixture on the Plaza since 1918. The decor—red leather banquettes, black Formica tables, tile floors, a coffered tin ceiling, and a 1940s-style service counter—hasn't changed much in the past half century. The food runs the gamut, from cashew mole enchiladas to New Mexico meat loaf to Mission-style burritos, but the ingredients tend toward southwestern. You'll rarely taste a better or spicier tortilla soup. You can cool it off with an old-fashioned ice cream treat from the soda fountain. All in all, it's a good stop for breakfast, lunch, or dinner. *54 Lincoln Ave., tel. 505/982–1664. Reservations not accepted. AE, D, MC, V.*

FRENCH

$$–$$$$ **ROCIADA.** Country French cooking is the bill of fare at this intimate bistro with soft lighting and a pressed-tin ceiling. Fresh ingredients are used for the Provençale specialties, including crayfish and escargots with a smoked-tomato saffron cream, and steak au poivre with spinach-mashed potatoes and Roquefort. The list of French wines is extensive. *304 Johnson St., tel. 505/983–3800. AE, D, MC, V. Closed Sun. No lunch.*

$$$ **315.** As if it were on a thoroughfare in Paris rather than on Old Santa Fe Trail, 315 has a Continental, white-tablecloth sophistication, but the offbeat wall art gives it a contemporary feel. Chef-owner Louis Moskow prepares refreshingly uncomplicated, Provençale-inspired fare using organic vegetables and locally raised meats. Seasonal specialties on the ever-evolving menu might include veal scallopini with chestnut sauce, and steak frites with béarnaise sauce and herb butter. The garden patio opens onto the street scene. There's an exceptional wine list. 315 Old Santa Fe Trail, tel. 505/986–9190. AE, MC, V. Closed Sun.

INDIAN

$–$$ **INDIA PALACE.** Even seasoned veterans of East Indian cuisine have
★ been known to rate this deep-pink, art-filled restaurant among the best in the United States. The kitchen prepares fairly traditional recipes—tandoori chicken, lamb vindaloo, *saag paneer* (spinach with farmer's cheese), shrimp *biryani* (tossed with cashews, raisins, almonds, and saffron rice)—but the presentation is always flawless and the ingredients fresh. Meals are cooked as hot or mild as requested. Try the Indian buffet at lunch. 227 Don Gaspar Ave. (enter from parking lot on Water St.), tel. 505/986–5859. AE, D, MC, V.

ITALIAN

$$–$$$ **ANDIAMO.** Produce from the farmers' market across the street adds to the seasonal surprises of this intimate northern Italian restaurant set inside a romantic cottage. Start with the crispy polenta with rosemary and Gorgonzola sauce; move on to the calamari pizza with fontina cheese, grilled onions, and bacon; and consider such hearty entrées as lasagna Bolognese or penne with merguez sausage, tomatoes, spinach, and roasted peppers. 322 Garfield St., near the Railyard, tel. 505/995–9595. AE, DC, MC, V. No lunch.

$$ **IL PIATTO.** Creative pasta dishes like risotto with duck, artichoke, and truffle oil and homemade pumpkin ravioli with pine nuts and brown sage butter grace the menu here. Entrées include roasted garlic–and–basil–stuffed duck breast with toasted almond jus. It's a crowded but nevertheless enjoyable trattoria with an informal ambience and a snug, urbane bar; the windows are dressed in frilly valances, and a mural of the Italian countryside lines one wall. 95 W. Marcy St., tel. 505/984–1091. AE, MC, V. No lunch weekends.

JAPANESE

$–$$ **MASA SUSHI.** Its linoleum floor, acoustic-tile ceilings, and a small dining room in a shopping center a short drive west of downtown might not raise your expectations that Masa serves the best sushi and Japanese fare in Santa Fe, but dig into a spicy scallop roll or fresh sea eel or sea urchin sushi, and you'll believe it. Shrimp tempura and *gyoza* (pork dumplings) are favorites from the "cooked" side of the menu. There's karaoke many weeknights. *Solana Center, 927 W. Alameda St., tel. 505/982–3334. MC, V. Closed Sun. No lunch Sat.*

MEDITERRANEAN

$–$$ ★ **WHISTLING MOON CAFE.** Unusual spices scent the inspired, mostly Mediterranean fare at this cozy spot, where specialties include chicken tagine, lamb shawarma, artichoke–grilled onion pizzas, and homemade walnut-mushroom ravioli. The coriander-cumin fries are irresistible, as is the homemade Moroccan-vanilla crème brûlée. Although the small ocher dining room with red Moroccan weavings is a touch noisy, the food and prices more than make up for it. *402 N. Guadalupe St., tel. 505/983–3093. MC, V. No lunch weekends.*

MEXICAN

$$–$$$ **EL ENCANTO.** A classy addition to the Guadalupe District, El Encanto was opened late in 2001 by the owner of Bert's la Taqueria, but here you'll generally find more upscale renditions of interior Mexican fare, including a full list of creative moles. The restaurant occupies a thick-walled adobe with a warren of romantic dining rooms hung with local art. Specialties include yellowfin tuna grilled with an agave-wine sauce and grilled pork loin baked with a pumpkin-seed salsa. *416 Agua Fria St., tel. 505/988–5991. AE, MC, V. Closed Sun.*

$–$$$ ★ **BERT'S LA TAQUERIA.** Salsa fans love this upbeat spot, where chips are served with six varieties of the hot stuff. The noisy dining room is filled with vintage Mexican movie posters and closely spaced tables that look back toward an open grill. The menu mixes the expected Mexican fare—enchiladas, soft tacos—with more unusual regional recipes. *1620 St. Michael's Dr., tel. 505/474–0791. AE, MC, V. Closed Sun.*

\$\$ OLD MEXICO GRILL. For a taste of Old Mexico in New Mexico, sample dishes like *arracheras* (the traditional Mexican name for fajitas) and tacos *al carbón* (shredded pork cooked in a mole sauce). Start the meal with a fresh ceviche appetizer and a cool lime margarita. It's a cozy spot with tile floors and wooden tables, a bit more charming than its shopping-center locale might suggest. *2434 Cerrillos Rd., College Plaza South, tel. 505/473–0338. Reservations not accepted. D, MC, V. No lunch weekends.*

PAN-ASIAN

\$\$ MU DU NOODLES. This warm and cozy eatery on an unfortunately busy stretch of Cerrillos Road excels both in its friendly and helpful staff and its superb pan-Asian fare. Book ahead on weekends—this place fills up fast. You can count on some great dinner specials each night, too. Sample shrimp pad Thai, tofu green curry, or house-marinated pork with rice vermicelli. *1494 Cerrillos Rd., tel. 505/988–1411. AE, MC, V. No lunch.*

\$–\$\$ KASASOBA. Maybe the best all-around Asian restaurant in Santa
★ Fe, this intimate, classy eatery behind the Sanbusco Center has just a handful of tables and specializes in both Japanese and Chinese noodle dishes. The *zaru soba* (cold buckwheat noodles with nori, wasabi, spring onions, and a dashi-shoyu dipping sauce) with tempura vegetables and shrimp is heavenly, as is the yellowfin tuna sashimi starter. Ramen and udon noodle specialties round out the menu, and there's a short but well-chosen wine list. *544 Agua Fria St., tel. 505/984–1969. AE, MC, V. No lunch Sat.–Mon.*

PIZZA

$ IL VICINO. This slick space a couple of blocks west of the Plaza, part of a local chain, serves exceptionally tasty wood-fired pizza, plus impressive salads, panini sandwiches, and a robust house-microbrewed ale, Wet Mountain I.P.A. Costs are low, in part because service is limited: you order your meal at the front desk, and they bring it out to you. The Angeli (roasted chicken, Portabello mushrooms, artichoke hearts, Gorgonzola, and balsamic marinara) is a winner among the 15 creatively topped pies. *321 W. San Francisco St., tel. 505/986–8700. AE, D, MC, V.*

SOUTHWESTERN

$$–$$$ GABRIEL'S. A great option near Pojoaque, perfect before the opera or on your way back to Santa Fe from points north, Gabriel's offers one of the best restaurant settings in the area: a spacious dining room with a Spanish-colonial theme, and a large flower-filled patio with candlelit tables. The main event here is the guacamole, prepared with great fanfare table-side. The margaritas are also stellar. Main dishes—steak fajitas, crab enchiladas—are less memorable but still usually quite good, and service is friendly but uneven. *U.S. 285/84, just north of Camel Rock Casino, 15 mi north of Santa Fe, tel. 505/455–7000. AE, D, DC, MC, V.*

$$–$$$ MARIA'S NEW MEXICAN KITCHEN. Maria's is proud to serve a whopping 100 kinds of margarita. All but six of the tequilas are 100% agave. This is also an excellent source of authentic New Mexican fare, including chiles rellenos, blue-corn enchiladas, and green-chile tamales. Strolling guitarists serenade the crowds most nights. *555 W. Cordova Rd., tel. 505/983–7929. AE, D, DC, MC, V.*

$–$$$ THE SHED. The lines at lunch attest to the status of this downtown New Mexican eatery. The rambling adobe dating from 1692 is decorated with folk art, and service is downright neighborly. Even if you're a devoted green chile fan, try the locally grown red chile the place is famous for. Specialties include red-chile enchiladas, green-chile stew with potatoes and pork, posole, and charbroiled

Shedburgers. The homemade desserts are fabulous. There's a full bar, too. 113½ E. Palace Ave., tel. 505/982–9030. AE, DC, MC, V. Closed Sun. No dinner Mon.–Wed.

$–$$ GUADALUPE CAFE. Come to this informal café for hefty servings of New Mexican favorites like enchiladas and quesadillas, topped off with *sopaipillas* (fluffy fried bread) and honey. The seasonal raspberry pancakes are one of many breakfast favorites. Service can be brusque and the wait for a table considerable. 422 Old Santa Fe Trail, tel. 505/982–9762. *Reservations not accepted. AE, D, DC, MC, V. Closed Mon. No dinner Sun.*

$ LA CHOZA. The far-less touristy, harder-to-find, and less expensive
★ sister to the Shed, La Choza arguably serves even better New Mexican fare. Chicken or pork *carne adovada* burritos, white-clam chowder spiced with green chiles, huevos rancheros, and wine margaritas are specialties. The dining rooms are dark and cozy, with vigas set across the ceiling and local art on the walls. The staff is friendly and competent, perhaps happy not to be contending with the hordes of tourists who frequent restaurants around the Plaza. 905 Alarid St., near Cerrillos Rd. at St. Francis Dr., tel. 505/982–0909. AE, DC, MC, V. Closed Sun.

SPANISH

$$$–$$$$ EL FAROL. In this crossover-cuisine town, owner David Salazar sums up his food in one word: "Spanish." Order a classic entrée like paella or make a meal from the nearly 30 different tapas—from tiny fried squid to wild mushrooms. Dining is indoors and out. Touted as the oldest continuously operated restaurant in Santa Fe, El Farol (built in 1835) has a relaxed ambience, a unique blend of the western frontier and contemporary Santa Fe. People push back the chairs and start dancing at around 9:30. The restaurant books outstanding live entertainment, mostly blues and jazz, and there's usually a festive flamenco performance weekly. 808 Canyon Rd., tel. 505/983–9912. D, DC, MC, V.

STEAK

$$–$$$$ **VANESSIE.** This classy, lodgelike space with high ceilings and a tremendously popular piano cabaret serves hefty portions of well-prepared chops and seafood. New Zealand rack of lamb, Australian cold-water rock lobster, and dry-aged steaks are among the specialties. There's lighter fare—burgers, onion loaf, salads—served in the piano bar, where noted musicians Doug Montgomery and Charles Tichenor perform classical and Broadway favorites well into the evening (no cover). *434 W. San Francisco St., tel. 505/982–9966. AE, DC, MC, V. No lunch.*

SHOPPING

Santa Fe has been a trading post for eons. A thousand years ago the great pueblos of the Chacoan civilizations were strategically located between the buffalo-hunting tribes of the Great Plains and the Indians of Mexico. Native Americans in New Mexico traded turquoise, which was thought to have magical properties, and other valuables with Indians from Mexico for metals, shells, parrots, and other exotic items. After the arrival of the Spanish and the subsequent development of the West, Santa Fe became the place to exchange silver from Mexico and natural resources from New Mexico—including hides, fur, and foodstuffs—for manufactured goods, whiskey, and greenbacks from the United States. With the building of the railroad in 1880, Santa Fe had access to all kinds of manufactured goods as well as those unique to the region via the old trade routes.

The trading legacy remains, but now downtown Santa Fe caters almost exclusively to those looking for handcrafted goods. Sure, T-shirt outlets and major retail clothing shops have moved in, but shopping in Santa Fe consists mostly of one-of-a-kind independent stores.

Santa Fe is a great place to window shop, perhaps because of the high visual standards such an artistic community commands. It is a town where color, texture, and pattern make a brave stand for diversity rather than uniformity. Canyon Road, where art galleries lie within a short distance of one another, is the perfect place to find one-of-a-kind gifts and collectibles. The downtown district, around the Plaza, has unusual gift shops, clothing, and shoe stores that range from theatrical to conventional, curio shops, and art galleries. The funky Guadalupe District, on the southwest perimeter of downtown, includes the Sanbusco Market Center. It's a laid-back neighborhood with a burgeoning restaurant and shopping scene, and it's far less touristy than the Plaza.

Farther out on Cerrillos Road, a traffic-jammed strip of shopping centers and chain motels, a new clutch of modern superstores has sprung up alongside Santa Fe's rather ordinary Villa Linda shopping mall. All the usual suspects are out here, around the intersection with Rodeo Road. On Cerrillos out by the I–25 exit, the inevitable **SANTA FE PREMIUM OUTLETS** (8380 Cerrillos Rd., at I–25, tel. 505/474–4000) contains about 35 shops, including Donna Karan, Coach, Bose, Dansk, and Brooks Brothers.

ART GALLERIES

The following are only a few of the nearly 200 galleries in greater Santa Fe—with the best of representational, nonobjective, Native American, Latin American, cutting-edge, photographic, and soulful works that defy categorization. The Santa Fe Convention and Visitors Bureau (☞ Visitor Information in Santa Fe A to Z, below) has a more extensive listing. The Wingspread Collectors Guide to Santa Fe and Taos is a good resource and is available in hotels and at some galleries, as well as on the Web at www.collectorsguide.com. Check the "Pasatiempo" pullout in the Santa Fe New Mexican on Friday for a preview of gallery openings.

ANDREW SMITH GALLERY (203 W. San Francisco St., tel. 505/ 984–1234) is a significant photo gallery dealing in works by

Edward S. Curtis and other 19th-century chroniclers of the American West. Other major figures are Ansel Adams, Eliot Porter, Laura Gilpin, Dorothea Lange, Alfred Stieglitz, Annie Liebowitz, and regional artists like Barbara Van Cleve.

DEWEY GALLERIES (Catron Building, 53 Old Santa Fe Trail, tel. 505/982–8632) shows historic Navajo textiles and jewelry, Pueblo pottery, and antique Spanish-colonial furniture, as well as paintings and sculpture (notably that of Allan Houser).

GERALD PETERS GALLERY (1011 Paseo de Peralta, tel. 505/954–5700) is Santa Fe's leading gallery of American and European art from the 19th century to the present. It has works by Max Weber, Albert Bierstadt, the Taos Society, the New Mexico Modernists, and Georgia O'Keeffe, as well as contemporary artists.

LEWALLEN CONTEMPORARY (129 W. Palace Ave., tel. 505/988–8997) is a leading center for a variety of contemporary arts by both southwestern and other acclaimed artists, among them Judy Chicago; sculpture, photography, ceramics, basketry, and painting are all shown in this dynamic space.

NEDRA MATTEUCCI GALLERIES (1075 Paseo de Peralta, tel. 505/982–4631; 555 Canyon Rd., tel. 505/983–2731) exhibits works by California regionalists, members of the early Taos and Santa Fe schools, and masters of American Impressionism and Modernism. Spanish-colonial furniture, Indian antiquities, and a fantastic sculpture garden are other draws of this well-respected establishment.

NIMAN FINE ARTS (125 Lincoln Ave., tel. 505/988–5091) focuses on the prolific work of contemporary Native American artist–Hopi painter Dan Namingha.

PHOTO-EYE GALLERY (376 Garcia St., tel. 800/227–6941) shows contemporary photography that includes the beautiful and sublime; there's also a stellar bookstore.

PLAN B EVOLVING ARTS (1050 Old Pecos Trail, tel. 505/982–1338) showcases young artists, with an emphasis on cutting-edge and avant-garde works, and presents provocative performance pieces.

SHIDONI FOUNDRY AND GALLERIES (Bishop's Lodge Rd., Tesuque, 5 mi north of Santa Fe, tel. 505/988–8001) casts work for accomplished and emerging artists from all over North America. On the grounds of an old chicken ranch, Shidoni has a rambling sculpture garden and a gallery. Self-guided tours are permitted Saturdays 9–5 and weekdays noon–1.

WYETH HURD GALLERY (839 Paseo de Peralta, tel. 505/989–8380) carries the work of the multigenerational arts family that includes N. C. Wyeth; his children Andrew, Carolyn, Ann, and Henriette Wyeth; Peter Hurd, Henriette's husband; Michael Hurd, son of Henriette and Peter; Jamie Wyeth, Andrew's son; and Peter de la Fuente, Henriette and Peter's grandson. Works include the landscape of the Delaware River valley that so inspired the Wyeth family and the New Mexico landscapes of Peter Hurd, who grew up in Roswell.

SPECIALTY STORES

Books

More than 20 stores in Santa Fe sell used books, and a handful of high-quality shops carry the latest releases from mainstream and small presses.

COLLECTED WORKS BOOK STORE (208B W. San Francisco St., tel. 505/988–4226) carries art and travel books, including a generous selection of books on southwestern art, architecture, and general history, as well as the latest in contemporary literature.

GARCIA STREET BOOKS (376 Garcia St., tel. 505/986–0151) is an outstanding independent shop strong on art, architecture, cookbooks, literature, and regional southwestern works—it's just a block from the Canyon Road galleries.

PHOTO-EYE BOOKS (376 Garcia St., tel. 505/988–5152) stocks new, rare, and out-of-print photography books.

Clothing

Women have been known to arrive here in Liz Claiborne and leave in a broomstick skirt and Navajo velvet shirt. Men who swore they never would don silver *bolo* ties. Function dictates form in cowboy fashions. A wide-brimmed hat is essential in open country for protection from heat, rain, and insects. Cowboy hats made by Resistol, Stetson, Bailey, and other leading firms cost between $30 and $500, and hats made of fur and other exotic materials can fetch four figures.

The pointed toes of cowboy boots slide easily into and out of stirrups, and high heels help keep feet in the stirrups. Tall tops protect ankles and legs on rides through brush and cactus country and can protect the wearer from a nasty shin bruise from a skittish horse.

Some western fashion accessories were once purely functional. A colorful bandanna protected an Old West cowboy from sun- and windburn and served as a mask in windstorms, when riding drag behind a herd or, on occasions far rarer than Hollywood would have us believe, when robbing trains. A cowboy's sleeveless vest enhanced his ability to maneuver during roping and riding chores and provided pocket space that his skintight pants—snug to prevent wrinkles in the saddle area—didn't. Belt buckles are probably the most sought-after accessories— gold ones go for as much as $1,000.

BACK AT THE RANCH (235 Don Gaspar, tel. 505/989–8110 or 888/962–6687) is a musty old shop stocked with used cowboy boots, from red leather to turquoise snakeskin, along with funky furniture, '50s-blanket coats, jewelry, and buckles. Some things get better with age, especially cowboy boots.

JANE SMITH (550 Canyon Rd., tel. 505/988–4775) sells extraordinary handmade western wear for women and men, from cowboy boots and sweaters to Plains Indians–style beaded tunics.

ORIGINS (135 W. San Francisco St., tel. 505/988–2323) borrows from many cultures, carrying pricey women's wear like antique kimonos and custom-dyed silk jackets. One-of-a-kind accessories complete the spectacular look that Santa Fe inspires.

Home Furnishings

ARTESANOS (222 Galisteo St.; 1414 Maclovia St.; tel. 505/471–8020) is one of the best Mexican-import shops in the nation, with everything from leather chairs to papier-mâché *calaveras* (skeletons used in Day of the Dead celebrations), tinware, and Talavera tiles.

COOKWORKS (322 S. Guadalupe St., tel. 505/988–7676), in the Guadalupe District, is really three excellent culinary shops in one: the first has cookware, the second cookbooks, and the third gourmet gifts and fancy prepared foods.

The **DESIGN CENTER** (418 Cerrillos Rd.) is a minimall of a dozen high-quality antiques shops (all with their own phone numbers).

DOODLET'S (120 Don Gaspar Ave., tel. 505/983–3771) has an eclectic collection of stuff: pop-up books, bizarre postcards, tin art, hooked rugs, and stringed lights. Wonderment is in every display case, drawing the eye to the unusual.

FOREIGN TRADERS (202 Galisteo St., tel. 505/983–6441), a Santa Fe institution founded as the Old Mexico Shop in 1927 and still run by the same family, stocks handicrafts, antiques, and accessories from Mexico and other parts of the world.

JACKALOPE (2820 Cerrillos Rd., tel. 505/471–8539), a legendary if somewhat overpriced bazaar, sprawls over 7 acres, incorporating several pottery barns, a furniture store, endless aisles of knickknacks from Latin America and Asia, and a huge greenhouse. There's a lunch counter, barnyard animals, and a prairie-dog village.

PACHAMAMA (223 Canyon Rd., tel. 505/983–4020) carries Latin American folk art, including small tin or silver *milagros*, the stamped metal images used as votive offerings. The shop also carries weavings and Spanish-colonial antiques.

Jewelry

KAREN MELFI COLLECTION (225 Canyon Rd., tel. 505/982–3032) sells high-quality yet moderately priced handmade jewelry and other wearable art.

ORNAMENT OF SANTA FE (209 W. San Francisco, tel. 505/983–9399) is full of cosmopolitan jewelry and unique hair accessories. Precious and semiprecious stones set in gold and silver push the envelope of tradition without being trendy.

Native American Arts and Crafts

CRISTOF'S (420 Old Santa Fe Trail, tel. 505/988–9881) has a large selection of pottery, sculpture, and contemporary Navajo weavings and sand paintings.

JOSHUA BAER & CO. (116½ E. Palace Ave., tel. 505/988–8944) carries superb historic Navajo textiles and rare antique Pueblo weavings.

MORNING STAR GALLERY (513 Canyon Rd., tel. 505/982–8187) is a veritable museum of Native American art and artifacts. An adobe shaded by a huge cottonwood tree houses antique basketry, pre-1940 Navajo silver jewelry, Northwest Coast Native American carvings, Navajo weavings, and art of the Plains Indians.

PACKARD'S ON THE PLAZA (61 Old Santa Fe Trail, tel. 505/983–9241), the oldest Native American arts-and-crafts store on Santa Fe Plaza, sells Zapotec Indian rugs from Mexico and original rug designs by Richard Enzer, old pottery, saddles, katsina dolls, and an excellent selection of coral and turquoise jewelry. Prices are quite high, but so are the standards.

The **RAINBOW MAN** (107 E. Palace Ave., tel. 505/982–8706), established in 1945, does business in the remains of a building that was damaged during the 1680 Pueblo Revolt. The shop carries early Navajo, Mexican, and Chimayó textiles, along with photographs by Edward S. Curtis, vintage pawn jewelry, and katsinas.

MARKETS
TESUQUE PUEBLO FLEA MARKET (U.S. 285/84, 7 mi north of Santa Fe, tel. 505/995–8626) was once considered the best flea market in America by its loyal legion of bargain hunters. The Tesuque Pueblo took over the market in the late '90s and raised vendor fees, which increased the presence of predictable, often pricey goods brought in by professional flea-market dealers. It remains a big shopping to-do, however, and you can still find everything from a half-wolf puppy or African carvings to vintage cowboy boots, fossils, or a wall clock made out of an old hubcap. The 12-acre market is next to the Santa Fe Opera and is open Friday–Sunday, mid-March–December.

Browse through the local produce, meat, flowers, honey, and cheese—much of it organic—at the **SANTA FE FARMERS MARKET** (Guadalupe St. by the Railyard, tel. 505/983–4098), which is held Tuesday and Saturday mornings from 7 'til noon, late April–November. It's a great people-watching event, and there's storytelling for kids.

OUTDOOR ACTIVITIES AND SPORTS

The Santa Fe National Forest is right in the city's backyard and includes the Dome Wilderness (5,200 acres in the volcanically formed Jemez Mountains) and the Pecos Wilderness (223,333 acres of high mountains, forests, and meadows at the southern end of the Rocky Mountain chain). The 12,500-ft Sangre de Cristo Mountains (the name translates as "Blood of Christ," for the red glow they radiate at sunset) fringe the city's east side, constant and gentle reminders of the mystery and power of the natural world. To the south and west, sweeping high desert is punctuated by several less formidable mountain ranges. The dramatic shifts in elevation and topography around Santa Fe make for a wealth of outdoor activities. Head to the mountains for fishing, camping, and skiing; to the nearby Rio Grande for kayaking and rafting; and almost anywhere in the area for bird-watching, hiking, and biking.

PARTICIPANT SPORTS

For a report on general conditions in the forest, contact the **SANTA FE NATIONAL FOREST OFFICE** (1474 Rodeo Rd., 87505, tel. 505/438–7840, www.fs.fed.us/r3/sfe). For a one-stop shop for information about recreation on public lands, which includes national and state parks, contact the **NEW MEXICO PUBLIC LANDS INFORMATION CENTER** (1474 Rodeo Rd., 87505, tel. 505/438–7542, fax 505/438–7582, www.publiclands. org). It has maps, reference materials, licenses, permits—just about everything you need to plan an adventure in the New Mexican wilderness.

Opened in 2001, the impressive **GENOVEVA CHAVEZ COMMUNITY CENTER** (3221 Rodeo Rd., tel. 505/955–4001) is a reasonably priced (adults $4 per day), top-notch facility with a regulation-size ice rink, an enormous gymnasium, indoor running track, 50-m pool, leisure pool with water slide and play structures, aerobics center, state-of-the-art fitness room, two racquetball courts, and a child-care center.

Bicycling

You can pick up a map of bike trips—among them a 30-mi round-trip ride from downtown Santa Fe to Ski Santa Fe at the end of NM 475—from the New Mexico Public Lands Information Center.

BIKE N' SPORT (1829 Cerrillos Rd., tel. 505/820–0809) provides rentals and information about guided tours. **SUN MOUNTAIN** (107 Washington Ave., tel. 505/820–2902) rents mountain bikes and offers a wide range of bike tours. The shop will also deliver to your hotel, any day, year-round.

Bird-Watching

At the end of Upper Canyon Road, at the mouth of the canyon as it wends into the foothills, the 135-acre **RANDALL DAVEY AUDUBON CENTER** harbors diverse birds and other wildlife. Guided nature walks are given many weekends; there are also two major hiking trails that you can tackle on your own. The home and studio of Randall Davey, a prolific early Santa Fe artist, can be toured on Monday afternoons in summer. A nature bookstore was added in 2002. *Upper Canyon Rd., tel. 505/983–4609, www.audubon.org/chapter/nm/nm/rdac. $2, house tour $5. Weekdays 9–5, weekends 10–4; grounds daily dawn–dusk.*

Fishing

There's excellent fishing spring through fall in the Rio Grande and the mountain streams that feed into it, as well as a short drive away along the Pecos River. **HIGH DESERT ANGLER** (435 S.

Guadalupe St., tel. 505/98–TROUT or 888/98–TROUT) is a superb fly-fishing outfitter and guide service. This is your one-stop for equipment rental, fly-fishing tackle, licenses, and advice.

Golf

MARTY SANCHEZ LINKS DE SANTA FE (205 Caja del Rio Rd., off NM 599 [the Santa Fe Relief Route], tel. 505/955–4400), an outstanding municipal facility with beautifully groomed 18- and 9-hole courses, sits on high prairie west of Santa Fe with fine mountain views. It has driving and putting ranges, a pro shop, and a snack bar. The greens fee is $49 for nonresidents on the 18-hole course, $30 on the par-3 9-holer.

The **TOWA GOLF RESORT** (Cities of Gold Casino Resort, 17746 U.S. 285/84, Pojoaque, tel. 505/455–9000 or 877/465–3489), 15 mi north of Santa Fe, was designed by pro legend Hale Irwin and sits in the foothills of the Sangre de Cristos, with stunning views of the Santa Fe ski basin and the Jemez Mountains over Los Alamos. The challenging 18-hole course opened in 2001; another 18 holes were slated to open in fall 2002. The greens fee is $49.

Hiking

Hiking around Santa Fe can take you into high-altitude alpine country or into lunaresque high desert as you head south and west to lower elevations. For winter hiking, the gentler climates to the south are less likely to be snow-packed, while the alpine areas will likely require snowshoes or cross-country skis. In summer, wildflowers bloom in the high country and the temperature is generally at least 10 degrees cooler than in town. The mountain trails accessible at the base of the Ski Santa Fe area (end of NM 475) stay cool on even the hottest summer days. Weather can change with one gust of wind, so be prepared with extra clothing, rain gear, food, and lots of water. Keep in mind that the sun at 10,000 ft is very powerful, even with a hat and sunscreen.

For information about specific hiking areas, contact the New Mexico Public Lands Information Center. The **SIERRA CLUB** (621 Old Santa Fe Trail, tel. 505/983–2703, riogrande.sierraclub.org/santafe/home.html) organizes group hikes of all levels of difficulty.

ASPEN VISTA is a lovely hike along a south-facing mountainside. Take Hyde Park Road (NM 475) 13 mi, and the trail begins before the ski area. After walking a few miles through thick aspen groves you'll come to panoramic views of Santa Fe. The path is well marked and gently inclines toward Tesuque Peak. The trail becomes shadier with elevation—snow has been reported on the trail as late as July. In winter, after heavy snows, the trail is great for intermediate to advanced cross-country skiing. The round-trip is 12 mi, but it's just 3½ mi to the spectacular overlook. The hillside is covered with golden aspen trees in late September.

TSANKAWI TRAIL, pronounced sank-ah-*wee*, will take you through the ancient rock trails of the Pajarito Plateau. In the 1½-mi loop you'll see petroglyphs and south-facing cave dwellings. Wear good shoes for the rocky path and a climb on a 12-ft ladder that shoots between a crevasse in the rock and the highest point of the mesa. *25 mi northwest of Santa Fe (take U.S. 285/84 north to the Los Alamos exit for NM 502; go west on 502 until the turnoff for White Rock, Hwy. 4; continue for several mi to the sign for Tsankawi on the left; the trail is clearly marked), tel. 505/672–3861.*

KASHA-KATUWE TENT ROCKS NATIONAL MONUMENT is a great choice if you have time for only one hike. The sandstone rock formations look like stacked tents in a stark, water- and wind-eroded box canyon. Located 45 minutes south of Santa Fe, near Cochiti Pueblo, Tent Rocks is excellent hiking year-round, although it can get hot in summer, when you should bring extra water. The drive to this magical landscape is equally awesome, as the road heads west toward Cochiti Dam and through the cottonwood groves around the pueblo. It's a good hike for kids. The round-trip hiking distance is only 2 mi, about 1½ hours, but it's the kind of place where you'll want to hang out for a while. Take a camera. *I–25 south to Cochiti exit 264 (follow NM 16 for 8 mi, turning right onto NM 22; continue approximately 3½ more mi past Cochiti Pueblo entrance; turn right on NM 266 "Tent Rocks" and continue 5 mi to the "*WELCOME TO TENT ROCKS*" sign; the last stretch of road is jarring, washboarded gravel), tel. 505/761–8700, www.nm.blm. gov/www/aufo/tent_rocks/tent_rocks.html. $5 per vehicle.*

Horseback Riding

New Mexico's rugged countryside has been the setting for many Hollywood westerns. Whether you want to ride the range that Gregory Peck and Kevin Costner rode or just head out feeling tall in the saddle, you can do so year-round. Rates average about $20 an hour.

BISHOP'S LODGE (Bishop's Lodge Rd., tel. 505/983–6377) provides rides and guides year-round. Call for reservations. Rides with **BROKEN SADDLE RIDING CO.** (off NM 14, Cerrillos, tel. 505/424–7774) take you around the old turquoise and silver mines the Cerrillos area is noted for. On a Tennessee Walker or a Missouri Fox Trotter you can explore the Cerrillos hills and canyons, 23 mi southeast of Santa Fe. This is not the usual nose-to-tail trail ride.

GALAROSA STABLE (NM 41, Galisteo, tel. 505/466–4654, www. galarosastables.com) provides rentals by the half- or full day south of Santa Fe in the panoramic Galisteo Basin.

Jogging

Because of the city's altitude (7,000–7,500 ft), you may feel heavy-legged and light-headed if you start running shortly after you arrive. Once you've become acclimated, though, you'll find that this is a great place to run. There's a jogging path along the Santa Fe River, parallel to Alameda, and another at Fort Marcy on Washington Avenue. The winding roads and paths up near the scenic campus of St. John's College are also ideal, although the terrain is quite hilly. Pick up gear and running advice at **RUNNING HUB** (333 Montezuma Ave., No. 6, tel. 505/820–2523); the store sponsors informal group runs many days—these are open to anybody.

River Rafting

If you want to watch birds and wildlife along the banks, try the laid-back Huck Finn floats along the Rio Chama or the Rio Grande's White Rock Canyon. The season is generally between April and September. Most outfitters have overnight package plans, and all offer half- and full-day trips. Be prepared to get wet, and wear secure water shoes. For a list of outfitters who guide trips on the Rio Grande and the Rio Chama, write the **BUREAU OF LAND MANAGEMENT (BLM), TAOS RESOURCE AREA OFFICE** (224 Cruz Alta Rd., Taos 87571, tel. 505/758–8851, www.nm.blm.gov/www/tafo/rafting/commercial.html), or stop by the BLM visitor center along NM 68 several miles south of Taos.

KOKOPELLI RAFTING ADVENTURES (541 Cordova Rd., tel. 505/983–3734 or 800/879–9035, www.kokopelliraft.com) specializes in trips through the relatively mellow White Rock Canyon as well as white water. **SANTA FE RAFTING COMPANY AND OUTFITTERS** (1000 Cerrillos Rd., tel. 505/988–4914 or 800/467–7238) customizes rafting tours. Tell them what you want—they'll do it.

Skiing

To save time during the busy holiday season you may want to rent skis or snowboards in town the night before hitting the slopes, or early in the morning so you don't waste any time paid for by your pricey lift ticket. **ALPINE SPORTS** (121 Sandoval St., tel. 505/983–5155) rents downhill and cross-country skis and snowboards. **COTTAM'S SKI RENTALS** (Hyde Park Rd., 7 mi northeast of downtown, toward Ski Santa Fe, tel. 505/982–0495) rents the works, including snowboards, sleds, and snowshoes.

SKI SANTA FE (end of NM 475, 18 mi northeast of downtown, tel. 505/982–4429; 505/983–9155 conditions; www.skisantafe.com), open roughly from late November through early April, is a fine, mid-size operation that receives an average of 225 inches of snow a year and plenty of sunshine. It's one of America's highest ski areas—the 12,000-ft summit has a variety of terrain and seems bigger than its 1,650 ft of vertical rise and 500 acres. There are some great powder stashes, tough bump runs, and many wide, gentle cruising runs. The 43 trails are ranked 20% beginner, 40% intermediate, and 40% advanced; there are seven lifts. Snowboarders are welcome, and there's the Norquist Trail for cross-country skiers. Chipmunk Corner provides day care and supervised kids' skiing. The ski school is excellent. Rentals, a good restaurant, a ski shop, and Totemoff Bar and Grill round out the amenities.

NIGHTLIFE AND THE ARTS

Santa Fe ranks among America's most cultured small cities. Gallery openings, poetry readings, plays, and dance concerts take place year-round, not to mention the famed opera and chamber-music festivals. Check the arts and entertainment listings in Santa Fe's daily newspaper, the *New Mexican* (www.sfnewmexican.com), particularly on Friday, when the arts and entertainment section, "Pasatiempo," is included, or check the weekly *Santa Fe Reporter* (www.sfreporter.com) for shows and events. Activities peak in the summer.

NIGHTLIFE

Culturally endowed though it is, Santa Fe has a pretty mellow nightlife scene, its key strength being live music, which is presented at numerous bars, hotel lounges, and restaurants. Austin-based blues and country groups and other acts wander into town, and members of blockbuster bands have been known to perform unannounced at small clubs while vacationing in the area. But on most nights your best bet might be quiet cocktails beside the flickering embers of a piñon fire or under the stars out on the patio.

DRAGON ROOM (406 Old Santa Fe Trail, tel. 505/983–7712), at the Pink Adobe restaurant, has been the place to see and be seen in Santa Fe for decades; flamenco and other light musical fare entertain at the packed bar.

ELDORADO COURT AND LOUNGE (309 W. San Francisco St., tel. 505/988–4455), in the lobby of the classy Eldorado Hotel, is a gracious lounge where classical guitarists and pianists perform nightly. It has the largest wines-by-the-glass list in town.

EL FAROL (808 Canyon Rd., tel. 505/983–9912) restaurant is where locals like to hang out. The roomy, somewhat ramshackle bar area has an old Spanish-western atmosphere, but you can order some fine Spanish brandies and sherries. On most nights you can listen to live flamenco, country, folk, or blues. Dancers pack the floor on weekend nights in summer.

EVANGELO'S (200 W. San Francisco St., tel. 505/982–9014) is an old-fashioned, smoky street-side bar, with pool tables, 200 types of imported beer, and rock bands on many weekends.

The city's largest dance club, **PARAMOUNT/BAR B** (331 Sandoval St., tel. 505/982–8999), has a snappy theme for each night of the week. The interior is contemporary and well lit and the dance floor is large. It's a good place to meet people, and it draws a gay-straight mix many evenings. There's also a Latin dance night, trash disco, and, on Friday, live music. In back, swanky Bar B is a cozy and somewhat quieter nook that usually has its own musical theme (and DJ). Cover charge varies.

SECOND STREET BREWERY (1814 2nd St., tel. 505/982–3030), a short drive south of downtown, packs in an eclectic, somewhat collegiate bunch for microbrewed ales, pretty good pub fare, and live rock and folk. There's an expansive patio, and the staff is friendly.

SWIG (135 W. Palace Ave., Level 3, tel. 505/955–0400), a trendy, upscale lounge that opened in spring 2002, has developed a loyal following for its chichi postmodern decor, rooftop patio, and well-dressed crowd. Drinks are expensive by Santa Fe standards, but that hasn't deterred many people.

THE ARTS

The performing arts scene in Santa Fe blossoms in summer. Classical or jazz concerts, Shakespeare on the grounds of St. John's campus, experimental theater at Santa Fe Stages, or flamenco—"too many choices!" is the biggest complaint. The rest of the year is a bit more quiet, but an increasing number of off-season venues have developed in recent years.

Concert Venues

Just a 10-minute drive north of town, **CAMEL ROCK CASINO** (U.S. 285/84, tel. 800/GO–CAMEL, www.camelrockcasino.com) presents relatively inexpensive pop and rock (Neil Sedaka, Pat Benatar, etc.) concerts.

Santa Fe's vintage downtown movie house was fully restored and converted into the 850-seat **LENSIC PERFORMING ARTS CENTER** (211 W. San Francisco St., tel. 505/988–1234, www. lensic.com) in 2001. The grand 1931 building, with Moorish and

Spanish Renaissance influences, hosts the Santa Fe Symphony, theater, classic films, lectures and readings, noted pop and jazz musicians, and many other noteworthy events.

Dance

The esteemed **ASPEN SANTA FE BALLET** (tel. 505/988–1234, www.aspensantafeballet.com) presents several ballet performances throughout the year at the Lensic Performing Arts Center.

Fans of Spanish dance should make every effort to see **MARIA BENITEZ TEATRO FLAMENCO** (Radisson Santa Fe, 750 N. St. Francis Dr., tel. 505/955–8562 or 888/435–2636, www.mariabenitez.com), who performs from late June through August at the Radisson Santa Fe. Maria Benitez is one of the world's premier flamenco dancers, and her performances often sell out well in advance.

Film

CINEMATHEQUE (1050 Old Pecos Trail, tel. 505/982–1338) screens foreign and independent films.

The intimate **JEAN COCTEAU** (418 Montezuma Ave., by the Sanbusco Center, tel. 505/988–2711) shows art films and has a pleasant little café.

Music

The acclaimed **SANTA FE CHAMBER MUSIC FESTIVAL** (tel. 505/982–1890, www.sfcmf.org) runs July through August, with performances nearly every night at either the Lensic Performing Arts Center or the St. Francis Auditorium. There are also free youth-oriented concerts given on several summer mornings.

SANTA FE OPERA (tel. 505/986–5900 or 800/280–4654, www.santafeopera.org) performs in a strikingly modern structure—a

2,126-seat, indoor-outdoor amphitheater with excellent acoustics and sight lines. Carved into the natural curves of a hillside 7 mi north of the city on U.S. 285/84, the opera overlooks mountains, mesas, and sky. Add some of the most acclaimed singers, directors, conductors, musicians, designers, and composers from Europe and the United States, and you begin to understand the excitement that builds every June. John Crosby directs the company, which presents five works in repertory each summer—a blend of seasoned classics, neglected masterpieces, and world premieres. Many evenings sell out far in advance, but inexpensive standing-room tickets are often available on the day of the performance.

The **SANTA FE SYMPHONY** (tel. 505/983–1414 or 800/480–1319, www.sf-symphony.org) performs eight concerts each season (from September to May) in the Lensic Performing Arts Center.

Orchestra and chamber concerts are given at St. Francis Auditorium and the Lensic Performing Arts Center by the **SANTA FE PRO MUSICA** (tel. 505/988–4640 or 800/960–6680, www.santafepromusica.com) from September through April. Baroque and other classical compositions are the normal fare; the annual Christmas and April's Bach Festival performances are highlights.

On the campus of the Santa Fe Indian School, the **PAOLO SOLERI OUTDOOR AMPHITHEATER** (1501 Cerrillos Rd., tel. 505/989–6300) hosts concerts spring–fall.

Theater

The oldest extant theater company west of the Mississippi, the **SANTA FE PLAYHOUSE** (142 E. De Vargas St., tel. 505/988–4262) occupies a converted 19th-century adobe stable and has been presenting an adventurous mix of avant-garde pieces, classical drama, and musical comedy since 1922. The Fiesta Melodrama—a spoof of the Santa Fe scene—runs late August–mid-September.

Internationally renowned **SANTA FE STAGES** (tel. 505/982–6683, www.santafestages.org) presents theater, dance, and music from late June to August; the company also presents shorter series from time to time. Performances are at the Lensic Performing Arts Center and **Firestone Plaza** (100 N. Guadalupe St.).

Several evenings and a few afternoons per week from mid-July through late August, **SHAKESPEARE IN SANTA FE** (tel. 505/982–2910, www.shakespearesantafe.org) presents performances of the Bard's finest at both the Lensic and in the courtyard of the John Gaw Meem Library at **St. John's College** (1160 Camino Cruz Blanca). When at St. John's campus, which occupies a magical setting in the city's east-side foothills, a performance of Renaissance music begins at 6, followed by the play at 7:30. It's best to get tickets in advance. Bring a picnic basket or buy food at the concession stand. It can get cold and the performers have been known to keep the show going in light rain. Tickets cost $15–$32. At St. John's, you can also opt to sit in the grass and watch for free; a $5 donation is suggested.

WHERE TO STAY

In Santa Fe you can ensconce yourself in quintessential Santa Fe style or anonymous hotel-chain decor, depending on how much you want to spend. Cheaper motels and hotels are on Cerrillos (pronounced sah-*ree*-yos) Road, which south of St. Francis Drive becomes a dreadfully traffic-clogged strip of could-be-anywhere fast-food and lodging chains. Quality varies greatly out on Cerrillos, but some of the best-managed and most attractive properties are (from most to least expensive) the Doubletree, the Courtyard Marriott, and the Motel 6. You'll pay a great deal more the closer you are to the Plaza, but for many visitors it's worth it to be within walking distance of many attractions. Some of the best deals are offered by B&Bs—many of those near the Plaza, while not cheap, still offer much better values than the big and inevitably touristy hotels. Rates drop considerably from November to April (excluding Thanksgiving and Christmas).

DOWNTOWN VICINITY

$$$$ **ELDORADO HOTEL.** The city's largest property sometimes gets a bad rap because it's the closest thing Santa Fe has to a convention hotel, but this is actually a highly inviting property with individually decorated rooms, a gracious staff, and some of the best mountain views of any downtown hotel. Rooms are stylishly furnished with carved southwestern-style desks and chairs, large upholstered club chairs, and art prints; many have terraces or kiva-style fireplaces. The rooftop pool and gym are great fun. The Old House restaurant is highly rated. There's music nightly, from classical Spanish guitar to piano, in the comfortable lobby lounge. Nearby, the inn rents out about 50 fully furnished apartments and condos with kitchens and as many as three bedrooms—these are ideal for longer stays or when traveling with friends or family. *309 W. San Francisco St., 87501, tel. 505/988–4455 or 800/955–4455, fax 505/ 995–4555, www.eldoradohotel.com. 201 rooms, 18 suites, 41 apartments, 10 condos. 2 restaurants, pool, health club, hot tub, massage, sauna, bar, lounge, shops, concierge, meeting rooms, parking (fee). AE, D, DC, MC, V.*

$$$$ **INN AT LORETTO.** This plush, oft-photographed, ancient pueblo–inspired property attracts a loyal clientele, many of whom swear by the friendly staff and high decorating standards. The lobby opens up to the gardens and pool, and leather couches and high-end architectural details make the hotel a pleasure to relax in. Rooms are among the largest of any downtown property and contain vibrantly upholstered handcrafted furnishings and sumptuous slate-floor bathrooms. The restaurant, Nellie's, serves estimable, creative southwestern fare. The Loretto opened a swank spa in summer 2002. Spa Blue offers a wide range of treatments, from desert sage massages to Decleor skin-care facials. *211 Old Santa Fe Trail, 87501, tel. 505/988–5531; 800/727–5531 outside New Mexico; fax 505/984–7988; www.hotelloretto.com. 140 rooms, 5 suites. Restaurant, pool, lounge, shops, meeting rooms, parking (fee). AE, D, DC, MC, V.*

downtown santa fe lodging

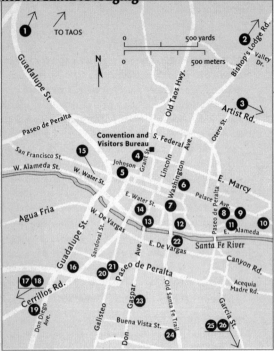

TO TAOS

Guadalupe St.

Bishop's Lodge Rd.

Valley Dr.

Paseo de Peralta

Artist Rd.

Old Taos Hwy.

Otero St.

San Francisco St.

W. Alameda St.

W. Water St.

Convention and Visitors Bureau

S. Federal Ave.

Johnson

Grant St.

Lincoln

Washington Ave.

E. Marcy

Agua Fria

W. De Vargas

Sandoval St.

E. Water St.

Palace Ave.

Paseo de Peralta

E. Alameda

E. De Vargas

Santa Fe River

Canyon Rd.

Guadalupe St.

Paseo de Peralta Ave.

Gaspar

Old Santa Fe Trail

Acequia Madre Rd.

Cerrillos Rd.

Don Diego Ave.

Galisteo

Buena Vista St.

Don

Garcia St.

N

0 — 500 yards
0 — 500 meters

Alexander's Inn, 10
Bishop's Lodge
Resort and Spa, 2
Don Gaspar
Inn, 23
El Farolito, 20
El Rey Inn, 18
Eldorado Hotel, 5
Garrett's Desert
Inn, 22
Grant Corner
Inn, 4

Hacienda del
Cerezo, 1
Hotel
St. Francis, 14
Hotel Santa Fe, 16
Inn at Loretto, 12
Inn of the
Anasazi, 6
Inn of the
Governors, 13
Inn of the
Turquoise Bear, 24

Inn on the
Alameda, 11
La Fonda, 7
La Posada de
Santa Fe Resort
and Spa, 8
Los Campos RV
Resort, 17
The Madeleine, 9
Pueblo Bonito
B&B Inn, 21

Rancheros de
Santa Fe
Campground, 26
Santa Fe Budget
Inn, 19
Santa Fe KOA, 25
Ten Thousand
Waves, 3
Water Street
Inn, 15

$$$$ ★ INN OF THE ANASAZI. Although it looks unassuming from the outside, this first-rate boutique hotel is one of Santa Fe's finest, with superb craftsmanship in every architectural detail. Each room has a beamed ceiling, kiva-style fireplace, antique Indian rugs, handwoven fabrics, and organic toiletries (including sunblock). Other amenities include full concierge services, twice-daily maid service, exercise bikes upon request, and a library with books on New Mexico and the Southwest. An especially nice touch in this desert town are the humidifiers in each guest room. A few deluxe rooms have balconies. The staff is thoroughly on top of things, and while this is an old building, it's been totally renovated. The restaurant is sublime, and hotel guests can dine in the romantic, candlelighted library. *113 Washington Ave., 87501, tel. 505/988–3030 or 800/688–8100, fax 505/988–3277, www.innoftheanasazi.com. 59 rooms. Restaurant, in-room safes, minibars, in-room VCRs, bar, library, parking (fee), some pets allowed (fee). AE, D, DC, MC, V.*

$$$$ LA FONDA. A rich history and charm are more prevalent in this sole Plaza-front hotel than first-class service and amenities. The present structure, built in 1922 and enlarged many times, captures the essence of authentic Santa Fe style——the pueblo-inspired architecture that defines the town today. Antiques and Native American art decorate the tiled lobby, and each room has hand-decorated wood furniture, wrought-iron light fixtures, and beamed ceilings. Some of the suites have fireplaces. The 14 rooftop rooms are the most luxurious and include Continental breakfast and private concierge services; there's also an exercise room, garden, and outdoor hot tub up here. There are plans to add a spa in 2003. La Plazuela Restaurant, with its hand-painted glass tiles, is a joy to sit in and serves quite good and creative southwestern food. Folk and Latin jazz bands rotate nightly in the bar. *100 E. San Francisco St., 87501, tel. 505/982–5511 or 800/523–5002, fax 505/988–2952, www.lafondasantafe.com. 143 rooms, 24 suites. Restaurant, pool, gym, 3 hot tubs, massage, 2 bars, laundry service, meeting rooms, parking (fee). AE, D, DC, MC, V.*

$$$$ LA POSADA DE SANTA FE RESORT AND SPA. In 1999 new owners undertook a massive renovation, transforming the Posada ("shelter") into an upscale, valet-parking-only hotel. Rooms here vary greatly in look and feel, from cozy and colorful to luxurious and high-ceilinged to dark and bare. Many rooms have fireplaces, beamed ceilings, and Native American rugs. Most of the accommodations are in a rambling adobe complex surrounding the main building; those in the older casitas, though authentic to their origins, seem cold and shabby and are the least desirable. The main building contains a handful of Victorian rooms with ceilings, marble accents in the bathrooms, and an old-world feel. The real stars here are the bar, the spa, and the common areas, including the wonderfully atmospheric Staab House Lounge off the lobby. The hotel's location, on a shaded stretch of Palace just blocks from the Plaza, is also ideal. Fuego restaurant specializes in world-beat contemporary fare. The resort and spa amenities are top-notch—$35 day passes are available for use of the spa, with individual treatments extra. *330 E. Palace Ave., 87501, tel. 505/986–0000 or 800/727–5276, fax 505/982–6850, www.laposadadesantafe. com. 120 rooms, 38 suites. Restaurant, pool, health club, hot tub, spa, steam rooms, bar, parking (fee). AE, D, DC, MC, V.*

$$$–$$$$ INN ON THE ALAMEDA. Near the Plaza and Canyon Road is one
★ of the Southwest's best small hotels. Alameda means "tree-lined lane," and this one perfectly complements the inn's location by the gurgling Santa Fe River. The adobe architecture and enclosed courtyards strewn with climbing rose vines combine a relaxed New Mexico country atmosphere with the luxury and amenities of a top-notch hotel. Rooms have a southwestern color scheme, handmade armoires and headboards, and ceramic lamps and tiles—many have patios and kiva fireplaces. The solicitous staff is first-rate. *303 E. Alameda St., 87501, tel. 505/984–2121 or 800/289–2122, fax 505/986–8756, www.innonthealameda.com. 59 rooms, 10 suites. Some refrigerators, gym, 2 hot tubs, massage, bar, library, laundry facilities, concierge, parking (free), meeting rooms, some pets allowed (fee). AE, D, DC, MC, V. CP.*

\$\$–\$\$\$\$ **GRANT CORNER INN.** The surrounding small garden and Victorian porch shaded by a huge weeping willow make this downtown Victorian B&B feel private. Antique Spanish and American country furnishings share space with potted greens and knickknacks. Room accents include old-fashioned fixtures, quilts, and Native American blankets. The ample breakfast, which is open to the public, includes home-baked breads and pastries, jellies, and blue-corn waffles. A separate nearby two-room hacienda can sleep seven. *122 Grant Ave., 87501, tel. 505/983–6678 or 800/964–9003, fax 505/983–1526, www.grantcornerinn.com. 9 rooms, 1 hacienda. Dining room, free parking; no kids under 8, no smoking. DC, MC, V. BP.*

\$\$\$ **EL FAROLITO.** All the beautiful southwestern and Mexican furniture in this small, upscale compound is custom-made, and all the art and photography original. Rooms are spacious with fireplaces and and separate entrances; some are in their own little buildings. El Farolito has a peaceful downtown location, just steps from the Capitol and a few blocks from the Plaza, and rooms are spacious and pleasant. Some have CD players. The same owners run the smaller Four Kachinas inn, which is close by and has one handicapped-accessible room (rare among smaller Santa Fe properties). *514 Galisteo St., 87501, tel. 505/988–1631 or 888/634–8782, www.farolito.com. 7 rooms, 1 suite. Some in-room VCRs; no smoking. AE, D, MC, V. CP.*

\$\$\$ **★** **HOTEL SANTA FE.** Picurís Pueblo maintains the controlling interest in this handsome Pueblo-style three-story hotel on the edge of the Guadalupe District and a short walk from the Plaza. The light and airy rooms and suites are done in traditional southwestern style, with locally handmade furniture, wooden blinds, and Pueblo paintings; many have balconies overlooking the city lights. The hotel gift shop, the only tribally owned store in Santa Fe, has lower prices than many nearby retail stores. The Corn Dance Cafe serves contemporary southwestern fare with many Native American ingredients and preparations—braised venison with sage and juniper in red wine is a specialty. Guests can learn about Native

American history and culture from informal talks held in the lobby, and Native American dances take place May–October. *1501 Paseo de Peralta, 87505, tel. 505/982–1200 or 800/825–9876, fax 505/984–2211, www.hotelsantafe.com. 40 rooms, 91 suites. Restaurant, some microwaves, pool, outdoor hot tub, massage, bar, laundry service, meeting rooms, concierge, free parking. AE, D, DC, MC, V.*

$$$ **INN OF THE GOVERNORS.** It looks like a glorified motor lodge from the outside, but this rambling hotel by the Santa Fe River has surprisingly characterful rooms and a young, enthusiastic staff. Rooms have a Mexican theme, with bright colors, hand-painted folk art, feather pillows, southwestern fabrics, and handmade furnishings; deluxe rooms also have balconies and fireplaces. New Mexican dishes and lighter fare like wood-oven pizzas are served in the restaurant, Mañana, which also books first-rate entertainers. *101 W. Alameda St., 87501, tel. 505/982–4333 or 800/234–4534, fax 505/989–9149, www.innofthegovernors.com. 100 rooms. Restaurant, room service, refrigerators, pool, bar, free parking, meeting rooms. AE, D, DC, MC, V. FP.*

$$–$$$ **DON GASPAR INN.** One of the city's best-kept secrets, this
★ exquisitely landscaped and decorated compound is on a pretty residential street a few blocks south of the Plaza. Its three historic houses have three distinct architectural styles: Arts and Crafts, Pueblo Revival, and Territorial. Floral gardens and aspen and cottonwood trees shade the tranquil paths and terraces, and both Southwest and Native American paintings and handmade furnishings enliven the sunny rooms and suites. The Arts and Crafts main house has two fireplaces, two bedrooms, and a fully equipped kitchen. Considering the setting and amenities, it's a great value. *623 Don Gaspar Ave., 87505, tel. 505/986–8664 or 888/986–8664, fax 505/986–0696, www.dongaspar.com. 4 rooms, 5 suites, 1 cottage. Some in-room hot tubs, some kitchens, refrigerators; no smoking. AE, MC, V. CP.*

$$–$$$ **HOTEL ST. FRANCIS.** Listed in the National Register of Historic Places, this three-story building, parts of which were constructed

in 1923, has walkways lined with turn-of-the-20th-century lampposts and is just one block south of the Plaza. The simple and elegant rooms with high ceilings, casement windows, brass-and-iron beds, marble and cherry antiques, and original artworks suggest a refined establishment, but the service has been known to fall short. Afternoon tea, with scones and finger sandwiches, is served daily (not complimentary) in the huge lobby, which rises 50 ft from a floor of blood-red tiles. The hotel bar is among the few places in town where you can grab a bite to eat until midnight. *210 Don Gaspar Ave., 87501, tel. 505/983–5700 or 800/529–5700, fax 505/989–7690, www.hotelstfrancis.com. 83 rooms. Restaurant, room service, bar, laundry service, free parking. AE, D, DC, MC, V.*

\$\$–\$\$\$ **INN OF THE TURQUOISE BEAR.** In the 1920s, poet Witter Bynner
★ played host to an eccentric circle of artists and intellectuals, as well as some wild parties in his mid-19th-century Spanish–Pueblo Revival home, which is now a B&B. Rooms are simple but have plush linens. The inn's style preserves the building's historic integrity, and there's plenty of ambience and a ranchlike lobby where you can stretch out or converse with other guests. You might sleep in the room where D. H. Lawrence and Frieda slept, or perhaps Robert Oppenheimer's room. The terraced flower gardens provide plenty of places to repose, away from the traffic on Old Santa Fe Trail, which borders the property. This is the quintessential Santa Fe inn. *342 E. Buena Vista, 87501, tel. 505/983–0798 or 800/396–4104, fax 505/988–4225, www.turquoisebear.com. 8 rooms, 2 with shared bath; 2 suites. In-room VCRs, library. AE, D, MC, V. CP.*

\$\$–\$\$\$ **WATER STREET INN.** The large rooms in this restored adobe 2½ blocks from the Plaza are decorated with reed shutters, antique pine beds, hand-stenciled artwork, and a blend of cowboy, Hispanic, and Native American art and artifacts. Most have fireplaces. Afternoon hors d'oeuvres are served in the living room. A patio deck is available for relaxing. The one drawback is that the inn overlooks a parking lot. *427 W. Water St., 87501, tel. 505/984–1193 or 800/646–6752, www.waterstreetinn.com. 8 rooms, 4 suites. In-room VCRs, outdoor hot tub, free parking. AE, DC, MC, V. CP.*

$–$$$ ALEXANDER'S INN. This two-story 1903 Craftsman-style house
★ in the Eastside residential area, a few blocks from the Plaza and
Canyon Road, exudes the charm of an old country inn. Rooms are
cozy and warm, with American country–style wooden furnishings,
family heirlooms, hand-stenciled walls, and dried-flower
arrangements. The grounds are dotted with tulips, hyacinths,
and lilac and apricot trees. There's also a pair of two-story cottages
with kitchens. The owners also run the seven-room Hacienda
Nicholas ($$–$$$), a small adobe house done in southwestern
style and with a more upscale look. Several of the Nicholas's
pleasant rooms with a mix of Provençal and Mexican furnishings
open onto a courtyard with fireplaces. *529 E. Palace Ave., 87501,
tel. 505/986–1431 or 888/321–5123, www.alexanders-inn.com. 5 rooms,
2 with shared bath; 2 cottages. Outdoor hot tub, free parking, some pets
allowed (fee); no TV in some rooms, no kids under 12 (except in cottages).
D, MC, V. CP.*

$$ PUEBLO BONITO B&B INN. Rooms in this adobe compound
built in 1873 have handmade and hand-painted furnishings,
Navajo weavings, sand paintings and pottery, locally carved
santos, and western art. All have kiva fireplaces and private
entrances, and many have kitchens. Breakfast is served in the main
dining room. Afternoon tea also offers complimentary margaritas.
The Plaza is a five-minute walk away. *138 W. Manhattan Ave., 87501,
tel. 505/984–8001 or 800/461–4599, fax 505/984–3155, www.
pueblobonitoinn.com. 13 rooms, 7 suites. Dining room, some kitchens, hot
tub, laundry facilities. AE, DC, MC, V. CP.*

$–$$ GARRETT'S DESERT INN. This sprawling, U-shape motor court
may surround a parking lot and offer relatively little in the way of
ambience, but it's well maintained and has an outstanding
location just a few blocks from the Plaza, smack in the middle of
historic Barrio de Analco. The clean, no-frills rooms are done in
earthy tones with a smattering of Southwest touches, and there's
a pleasant pool and patio. *311 Old Santa Fe Trail, 87501, tel. 505/*

982–1851 or 800/888–2145, www.garrettsdesertinn.com. 82 rooms. Pool, billiards, lounge, car rental, free parking. AE, DC, MC, V. CP.

$–$$ **THE MADELEINE.** Carolyn Lee, who owns Alexander's Inn, has named her successful establishments after her children. The Madeleine is the only Queen Anne–style house in the city, three blocks east of the Plaza in a quiet garden setting. The public rooms in this 1886 building are open and sunny, with genuine Queen Anne style. This is arguably the most romantic of Lee's inns, at least if Victoriana is your thing. Four of the rooms have fireplaces; the third-floor room has wonderful mountain views and a spiral staircase to the garden. Other touches include stained-glass windows, lace curtains, and fresh-cut flowers. You'll feel as if you've made a genteel step back in time. 106 Faithway St., 87501, tel. 505/986–1431 or 888/321–5123, www.madeleineinn.com. 6 rooms, 2 with shared bath; 2 cottages. No kids under 12 (except in cottages), no smoking. AE, D, MC, V. BP.

$ **SANTA FE BUDGET INN.** On the southern edge of the Railyard District, this inn offers affordable low-frills comfort and standard southwestern decor within walking distance of the Plaza (six blocks). Special packages are available for three- and four-day stays during peak-season events. 725 Cerrillos Rd., 87501, tel. 505/982–5952, fax 505/984–8879, www.santafebudgetinn.com. 160 rooms. Restaurants, pool, free parking. AE, DC, MC, V. CP.

LOWER CERRILLOS ROAD

$–$$ **EL REY INN.** The tree-shaded, whitewashed El Rey has been a Santa Fe landmark motel for 65 years. Rooms are decorated in southwestern, Spanish colonial, and Victorian style. Some have kitchenettes and fireplaces. The largest suite, with seven rooms, sleeps six and has antique furniture, a full kitchen, a breakfast nook, and two patios. Service is friendly. 1862 Cerrillos Rd., 87505, tel. 505/982–1931 or 800/521–1349, fax 505/989–9249. 79 rooms, 8 suites. Some kitchenettes, pool, 2 hot tubs, sauna, playground, laundry facilities. AE, DC, MC, V. CP.

NORTH OF SANTA FE

$$$$ **BISHOP'S LODGE RESORT AND SPA.** This resort established in
★ 1918 is in a bucolic valley at the foot of the Sangre de Cristo
Mountains and yet only a five-minute drive from the Plaza. Behind
the main building is an exquisite chapel that was once the private
retreat of Archbishop Jean Baptiste Lamy. Outdoor activities
include hiking, horseback riding, organized trail riding (with
meals) into the adjacent national forest, skeet-shooting, and
trapshooting. The two lodge buildings have antique southwestern
furnishings—shipping chests, tinwork from Mexico, and Native
American and western art; most of the rooms, in other buildings
scattered around the property, have less character, though some
rooms have fireplaces. The lodge has a state-of-the-art spa and
good fitness facilities. The restaurant, specializing in inventive
Nuevo Latino fare, serves a bountiful Sunday brunch, probably
the best in Santa Fe. Although Bishop's is among the priciest
hotels in town, the off-season discounts are as steep as 65%.
*Bishop's Lodge Rd., 2½ mi north of downtown, 87501, tel. 505/983–6377
or 800/732–2240, fax 505/989–8739, www.bishopslodge.com. 92
rooms, 19 suites. 2 restaurants, some refrigerators, 4 tennis courts, pool,
gym, hot tub, massage, spa, fishing, hiking; horseback riding, bar, children's
programs (ages 4–12), business services, meeting rooms, airport shuttle,
free parking. AE, D, MC, V.*

$$$$ **HACIENDA DEL CEREZO.** Stop reading here if $600 is more than
★ you want to spend on a room. Keep in mind that the rate includes
three meals for two people prepared by a master chef; dinner is
a five-course candlelit affair in the great room or in the courtyard,
looking out onto the vanishing-edge pool and the desert beyond.
The inn sits on a splendidly isolated patch of land 25 minutes
northwest of downtown. Rooms are subtly executed in prints,
ornaments, carvings on the beams of the viga ceilings, and
etchings in the glass shower doors. Each room has a king-size bed,
a generous sitting area, a kiva fireplace, an enclosed patio, and
a view of the mountains. Service is gracious and understated. *100
Camino del Cerezo, 87501, tel. 505/982–8000 or 888/982–8001, fax*

505/983–7162, www.haciendadelcerezo.com. 10 rooms. Restaurant, tennis court, pool, outdoor hot tub, hiking, horseback riding, free parking; no kids. AE. FAP.

$$$–$$$$ ★ **TEN THOUSAND WAVES.** Devotees appreciate the Zenlike atmosphere of this Japanese-style health spa and small hotel above town. Eight cozy hillside cottages tumble down a piñon-covered hill below the first-rate spa, which is tremendously popular with day visitors. The sleek, uncluttered accommodations have marble or stone wood-burning fireplaces, CD stereos, fine woodwork, low-slung beds or futons, and courtyards or patios; two come with full kitchens. The facility has private and communal indoor and outdoor hot tubs and spa treatments. Private tubs run from $20 per hour, communal tubs from $14 for an unlimited time; massage and spa treatments cost from $45 to $205. Overnight guests can use the communal tubs for free. The snack bar serves sushi and other healthful treats. *3451 Hyde Park Rd., 4 mi from the Plaza (Box 10200, 87501), tel. 505/982–9304, fax 505/989–5077, www.tenthousandwaves.com. 8 cottages. Snack bar, some kitchens, refrigerators, some in-room VCRs, 9 outdoor hot tubs, massage, spa, shop, some pets allowed (fee), free parking; no TV in some rooms. D, MC, V.*

CAMPING

LOS CAMPOS RV RESORT. The only full-service RV park lies between a car dealership on one side and open vistas on the other. Poplars and Russian olive trees, a dry riverbed, and mountains rise in the background. *3574 Cerrillos Rd., tel. 505/473–1949 or 800/852–8160. Flush toilets, full hook-ups, dump station, drinking water, electricity, laundry, grills, picnic tables, public phone, playground, pool. 95 sites. $25–$33. MC, V.*

RANCHEROS DE SANTA FE CAMPGROUND. This 22-acre camping park is on a hill in the midst of a piñon forest. Bring your tent or RV, or rent a cabin. You can get LP gas service here. An Internet station and cable TV hook-ups were added in 2002; other amenities include nightly movies in summer, a hiking

Your Checklist for a Perfect Journey

WAY AHEAD
- Devise a trip budget.
- Write down the five things you want most from this trip. Keep this list handy before and during your trip.
- Make plane or train reservations. Book lodging and rental cars.
- Arrange for pet care.
- Check your passport. Apply for a new one if necessary.
- Photocopy important documents and store in a safe place.

A MONTH BEFORE
- Make restaurant reservations and buy theater and concert tickets. Visit fodors.com for links to local events.
- Familiarize yourself with the local language or lingo.

TWO WEEKS BEFORE
- Replenish your supply of medications.
- Create your itinerary.
- Enjoy a book or movie set in your destination to get you in the mood.

- Develop a packing list. Shop for missing essentials. Repair and launder or dry-clean your clothes.

A WEEK BEFORE
- Stop newspaper deliveries. Pay bills.
- Acquire traveler's checks.
- Stock up on film.
- Label your luggage.
- Finalize your packing list— take less than you think you need.
- Create a toiletries kit filled with travel-size essentials.
- Get lots of sleep. Don't get sick before your trip.

A DAY BEFORE
- Drink plenty of water.
- Check your travel documents.
- Get packing!

DURING YOUR TRIP
- Keep a journal/scrapbook.
- Spend time with locals.
- Take time to explore. Don't plan too much.

trail, and a recreation room. *Old Las Vegas Hwy. (Exit 290 from I–25, 10½ mi south of the Plaza), tel. 505/466–3482 or 800/426–9259, www.rancheros.com. Flush toilets, full hook-ups, dump station, drinking water, laundry facilities, showers, grills, picnic tables, electricity, public telephone, general store, playground, pool. 37 tent sites, 95 RV sites, 5 cabins. Tent sites $15–$17, water and electric hook-ups $19–$23, full hook-ups $22–$27, cabins $30–$33. MC, V. Mid-Mar.–Oct.*

SANTA FE KOA. In the foothills of the Sangre de Cristo Mountains, 20 minutes southeast of Santa Fe, this large campground with tent sites, RV sites, and cabins is covered with piñons, cedars, and junipers. Internet access is available; activities include basketball, ring toss, video games, and free movies. *Old Las Vegas Hwy. (Box 95-A, 87505), tel. 505/466–1419 or 800/562–1514, www.koa.com/where/nm/31159.htm. Flush toilets, partial hook-ups (electric), drinking water, laundry facilities, showers, fire grates, fire pits, picnic tables, electricity, public phone, general store. 44 RV sites, 26 tent sites, 10 cabins. Tent sites $22–$25, RV sites $26–$31, cabins $38–$40. D, MC, V. Mar.–Oct.*

In This Chapter

Updated by Andrew Collins

side trips
from santa fe

YOU CAN HARDLY GRASP THE PROFUNDITY of New Mexico's ancient past or its immense landscape without journeying into the hinterland. Each of the excursions below can be accomplished in a day or less, but in the cases of Abiquiu and Los Alamos it's worth considering an overnight. The High Road to Taos is a very full day, so start early or plan on spending the night near or in Taos.

PUEBLOS NEAR SANTA FE

This trip will take you to several of the state's 19 pueblos, including San Ildefonso, one of the state's most picturesque, and Santa Clara, whose lands harbor a dramatic set of ancient cliff dwellings. Between the two reservations sits the ominous landmark called Black Mesa, which you can see from NM 30 or NM 502. The solitary butte has inspired many painters, including Georgia O'Keeffe. Plan on spending one to three hours at each pueblo, and leave the day open if you are there for a feast day, when dances are set to an organic rather than mechanical clock. Pueblo grounds and hiking areas do not permit pets.

Pojoaque Pueblo

24 *17 mi north of Santa Fe on U.S. 285/84.*

There is not much to see in the pueblo's plaza area, which hardly has a visible core, but the state visitor center and adjoining **Poeh**

Cultural Center and Museum on U.S. 285/84 are worth a visit. The latter is an impressive complex of traditional adobe buildings, including the three-story Sun Tower, which contains a museum, a cultural center, and artists' studios. There are frequent demonstrations by artists, exhibitions, and, on Saturday from May through September, traditional ceremonial dances. By the early 20th century the pueblo was virtually uninhabited, but the survivors eventually began to restore it. Pojoaque's feast day is celebrated with dancing on December 12. The visitor center is one of the friendliest and best stocked in northern New Mexico, with free maps and literature on hiking, fishing, and the area's history. The crafts shop in the visitor center is one of the most extensive among the state's pueblos; it carries weaving, pottery, jewelry, and other crafts by both Pojoaque and other indigenous New Mexicans. The pueblo also operates the adjacent **Cities of Gold Resort,** which comprises a casino, 124-room hotel, sports bar and simulcast; Towa Golf Resort, and several shops and restaurants. U.S 285/84, 17 mi *north of Santa Fe, tel. 505/455–3460, www.citiesofgold.com. Free. Apr.–Dec., Mon.–Sat. 9–6, Sun. 10–4; Jan.–Mar., Mon.–Sat. 9–5:30, Sun. 10–4. Sketching, cameras, and video cameras prohibited, except during Sat. Native American dances.*

San Ildefonso Pueblo

25 *23 mi north of Santa Fe via U.S. 285/84 to NM 502 west.*

Maria Martinez, one of the most renowned Pueblo potters, lived here. She first created her exquisite "black on black" pottery in 1919 and in doing so sparked a major revival of all Pueblo arts and crafts. She died in 1980, and the 26,000-acre San Ildefonso Pueblo remains a major center for pottery and other arts and crafts. Many artists sell from their homes, and there are trading posts, a visitor center, and a museum where some of Martinez's work can be seen on weekdays. San Ildefonso is also one of the more visually appealing pueblos, with a well-defined plaza core

side trips from santa fe

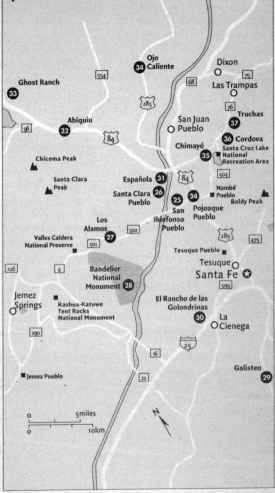

and a spectacular setting beneath the Pajarito Plateau and Black Mesa. The pueblo's feast day is January 23, when unforgettable buffalo, deer, and Comanche dances are performed from dawn to dusk. Cameras are not permitted at any of the ceremonial dances but may be used at other times with a permit. *NM 502, tel. 505/455–3549. $3 per vehicle, still-camera permit $10, video recorder permit $20, sketching permit $15. Daily 8–4.*

Santa Clara Pueblo

26 *27 mi northwest of Santa Fe, 10 mi north of San Ildefonso Pueblo via NM 30.*

Santa Clara Pueblo, southwest of Española, is the home of a historic treasure—the awesome **Puyé Cliff Dwellings** (open June–August, daily 8–7), believed to have been built in the 13th to 14th centuries. They can be seen by driving 9 mi up a gravel road through a canyon, south of the village off NM 502. The pueblo also contains four ponds, miles of stream fishing, and picnicking and camping facilities. You can tour the cliff dwellings, topped by the ruins of a 740-room pueblo, on your own or with a guide. Permits for the use of trails, camping, and picnic areas, as well as for fishing in trout ponds, are available at the sites; recreation areas are open April–October, dawn–dusk.

Shops in the village sell burnished red pottery, engraved blackware, paintings, and other arts and crafts. All pottery is made via the coil method, not with a pottery wheel. Santa Clara is known for its carved pieces, and Avanyu, a water serpent that guards the waters, is the pueblo's symbol. Other typical works include engagement baskets, wedding vessels, and seed pots. The pueblo's feast day of St. Claire is celebrated on August 12. *Off NM 502 on NM 30, Española, tel. 505/753–7326. Pueblo free, cliff dwellings $5, video and still-camera permits $15. Daily 8–4:30.*

JEMEZ COUNTRY

In the Jemez region, the 1,000-year-old Anasazi ruins at Bandelier National Monument present a vivid contrast to Los Alamos National Laboratory, birthplace of the atomic bomb. You can easily take in part of Jemez Country in a day trip from Santa Fe.

On this tour you can see terrific views of the Rio Grande valley, the Sangre de Cristos, the Galisteo Basin, and, in the distance, the Sandias. There are places to eat and shop for essentials in Los Alamos and a few roadside eateries along NM 4 in La Cueva and Jemez Springs. There are also numerous turnouts along NM 4, several which have paths leading down to the many excellent fishing spots along the Jemez River.

The 48,000-acre Cerro Grande fire of May 2000 burned much of the pine forest in the lower Jemez Mountains, as well as more than 250 homes in Los Alamos. Parts of the drive are still scarred with charcoaled remains, but a considerable amount of vegetation has returned.

Los Alamos

27 *35 mi from Santa Fe via U.S. 285/84 north to NM 502 west.*

Look at old books on New Mexico and you'll rarely find a mention of Los Alamos, now a busy town of 18,500 that has the highest per capita income in the state. Like so many other communities in the Southwest, Los Alamos was created expressly as a company town; only here the workers weren't mining iron, manning freight trains, or hauling lumber—here, for at least the first two decades, most residents were busy toiling at America's foremost nuclear research facility, Los Alamos National Laboratory (LANL). The facility still employs some 10,000 area workers.

Just a few miles from ancient cave dwellings, scientists led by a morally conflicted J. Robert Oppenheimer built Fat Man and Little Boy, the atom bombs that in August 1945 decimated Hiroshima and Nagasaki, respectively. LANL was created in 1943 under the auspices of the intensely covert Manhattan Project, whose express purpose it was to expedite an Allied victory during World War II. Indeed, Japan surrendered—but a full-blown Cold War between Russian and the United States ensued for another 4½ decades.

LANL works hard today to promote its broader platforms, including "enhancing global nuclear security" but also finding new ways to detect radiation, fighting pollution and environmental risks associated with nuclear energy, and furthering studies of the solar system, biology, and computer sciences. Similarly, the town of Los Alamos now strives to be more well rounded, better understood, and tourist-friendly.

The **BRADBURY SCIENCE MUSEUM** is Los Alamos National Laboratory's public showcase, and its exhibits offer a surprisingly balanced and provocative examination of such thorny topics as atomic weapons and nuclear power. You can experiment with lasers; witness research in solar, geothermal, fission, and fusion energy; learn about DNA fingerprinting; and view exhibits about World War II's Project Y (the Manhattan Project, whose participants developed the atomic bomb). *Los Alamos National Laboratory, 15th St. and Central Ave., tel. 505/667–4444, www.lanl.gov/external/museum. Free. Tues.–Fri. 9–5, Sat.–Mon. 1–5.*

The New Mexican architect John Gaw Meem designed the **FULLER LODGE,** a short drive up Central Avenue from the Bradbury Science Museum. The massive log building was erected in 1928 as a dining and recreation hall for a small private boys' school. In 1942 the federal government purchased the school and made it the base of operations for the Manhattan Project. Part of the lodge is an art center that shows the works of northern New Mexican artists; there's a picturesque rose garden on the grounds. 2132

Central Ave., tel. 505/662–9331, www.losalamos.org/flac.html. Free. Mon.–Sat. 10–4.

The **LOS ALAMOS HISTORICAL MUSEUM,** in a log building adjoining Fuller Lodge, displays exhibits on the once-volatile geological history of the volcanic Jemez Mountains, the 700-year history of human life in this area, and more on—you guessed it— the Manhattan Project. It's rather jarring to observe ancient Anasazi potsherds and arrowheads in one display and photos of an obliterated Nagasaki in the next. 1921 Juniper St., tel. 505/662– 4493, www.losalamos.com/historicalsociety/museum.asp. Free. Oct.– Apr., Mon.–Sat. 10–4, Sun. 1–4; May–Sept., Mon.–Sat. 9:30–4:30, Sun. 11–5.

WHERE TO EAT AND STAY

$–$$ **HILL DINER.** With a friendly staff and clientele, this large diner serves some of the finest burgers in town, along with chicken-fried steaks, homemade soups, and heaps of fresh vegetables. 1315 Trinity Dr., tel. 505/662–9745. AE, D, DC, MC, V.

$ **LOS ALAMOS INN.** Rooms in this one-story hotel have modern southwestern decor and sweeping canyon views. Tommy's, the inn's restaurant and bar, serves American and southwestern regional specialties; the Sunday brunch is popular. 2201 Trinity Dr., 87544, tel. 505/662–7211 or 800/279–9279, fax 505/661–7714, www. losalamosinn.com. 115 rooms. Restaurant, pool, some refrigerators, some kitchenettes, business services, bar, meeting room. AE, D, DC, MC, V.

$ **BEST WESTERN HILLTOP HOUSE HOTEL.** Minutes from the Los Alamos National Laboratory, this hotel hosts both vacationers and scientists. All the rooms are furnished in modern southwestern style; deluxe ones have kitchenettes. 400 Trinity Dr. (Box 250, 87544), tel. 505/662–2441 or 800/462–0936, fax 505/662–5913, www.bestwesternlosalamos.com. 87 rooms, 13 suites. Restaurant, room service, refrigerators, indoor pool, gym, hot tub, lounge, laundry facilities, meeting rooms. AE, D, DC, MC, V. CP.

$ RENATA'S ORANGE STREET BED & BREAKFAST. Linda Hartman is the proprietor of this B&B. In an unremarkable 1948 wood-frame house in a quiet residential neighborhood, rooms are furnished in southwestern and country style. The public area has cable TV and a VCR, and you can use the kitchen and the laundry; rooms also have high-speed DSL access. *3496 Orange St., 87544, tel./fax 505/662–2651 or 800/662–3180, www.losalamos.com/orangestreetinn. 6 rooms, 2 with bath; 3 suites. In-room data ports, some refrigerators, laundry facilities, business services. AE, D, DC, MC, V. BP.*

Bandelier National Monument

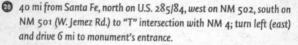

28 *40 mi from Santa Fe, north on U.S. 285/84, west on NM 502, south on NM 501 (W. Jemez Rd.) to "T" intersection with NM 4; turn left (east) and drive 6 mi to monument's entrance.*

Seven centuries before the Declaration of Independence was signed, compact city-states existed in the Southwest. Remnants of one of the most impressive of them can be seen at **Frijoles Canyon** in Bandelier National Monument. At the canyon's base, beside a gurgling stream, are the remains of cave dwellings, ancient ceremonial kivas, and other stone structures that stretch out for more than a mile beneath the sheer walls of the canyon's tree-fringed rim. For hundreds of years the Anasazi people, relatives of today's Rio Grande Pueblo Indians, thrived on wild game, corn, and beans. Suddenly, for reasons still undetermined, the settlements were abandoned.

Wander through the site on a paved, self-guided trail. If you can climb steep wooden ladders and squeeze through narrow doorways, you can explore some of the cave dwellings and cell-like rooms.

Bandelier National Monument, named after author and ethnologist Adolph Bandelier (his novel *The Delight Makers* is set in Frijoles Canyon), contains 23,000 acres of backcountry wilderness, waterfalls, and wildlife. Sixty miles of trails traverse the park. A small museum in the visitor center focuses on the area's prehistoric and contemporary Native American cultures, with displays of artifacts from 1200 to modern times. *tel. 505/ 672–0343, www.nps.gov/band. $10 per vehicle, good for 7 days. Summer, daily 8–6; spring and fall, daily 8–5:30; winter, daily 8–4:30.*

Galisteo

29 *25 mi south of Santa Fe via I–25 north to U.S. 285 south to NM 41 south.*

South of Santa Fe lie the immense open spaces of the sublime Galisteo Basin and the quintessential New Mexican village of Galisteo—a harmonious blend of multigenerational New Mexicans and recent migrants who protect and treasure the bucolic solitude of their home. The drive from Santa Fe takes about 30 minutes and offers a panoramic view of the surreal, sculpted landscape of the Galisteo Basin, which is an austere contrast to the alpine country of the Sangre de Cristos. It's a good place to go for a leisurely lunch or a sunset drive to dinner, maybe with horseback riding or a day of lounging and having body treatments at the local spa, Vista Clara Ranch.

Founded as a Spanish outpost in 1614 and built largely with rocks from nearby Pueblo ruins, Galisteo is a village with many artists and equestrians (trail rides and rentals are available at local stables). Cottonwood trees shade the low-lying pueblo-style architecture, a premier example of vernacular use of adobe and stone. The small church is open only for Sunday services. The excellent gallery **LINDA DURHAM CONTEMPORARY ART** (tel. 505/466–6600) exhibits sculpture and paintings from mainly New Mexican artists. Aside from the inn, spa-resort, and the gallery, a *tiendita*, a small store that sells bare essentials, constitutes the commercial center of Galisteo.

WHERE TO STAY

$$$$ **VISTA CLARA RANCH RESORT AND SPA.** On the edge of Galisteo,
★ this hideaway on 80 acres combines modern spa amenities and

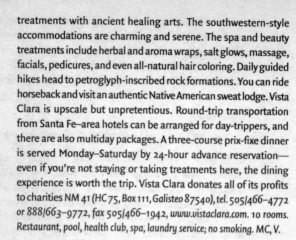
treatments with ancient healing arts. The southwestern-style accommodations are charming and serene. The spa and beauty treatments include herbal and aroma wraps, salt glows, massage, facials, pedicures, and even all-natural hair coloring. Daily guided hikes head to petroglyph-inscribed rock formations. You can ride horseback and visit an authentic Native American sweat lodge. Vista Clara is upscale but unpretentious. Round-trip transportation from Santa Fe–area hotels can be arranged for day-trippers, and there are also multiday packages. A three-course prix-fixe dinner is served Monday–Saturday by 24-hour advance reservation— even if you're not staying or taking treatments here, the dining experience is worth the trip. Vista Clara donates all of its profits to charities NM 41 (HC 75, Box 111, Galisteo 87540), tel. 505/466–4772 or 888/663–9772, fax 505/466–1942, *www.vistaclara.com*. 10 rooms. *Restaurant, pool, health club, spa, laundry service; no smoking. MC, V.*

$$–$$$ ★ **THE GALISTEO INN.** In the center of Galisteo, this rambling old adobe hacienda has been deftly transformed into an idyllic inn. Thick adobe walls, wide-plank pine floors worn with age and rich in patina, and vistas and patios from which to enjoy them add to the privacy and romance of this refuge. The restaurant ($$$) is acclaimed for its innovative American cuisine (reservations essential). The menu changes often and might feature roasted veal chop stuffed with prosciutto, sage, and fresh mozzarella with a port-wine glaze. 9 La Vega (HC 75, Box 4, Galisteo 87540), tel. 505/466–8200, fax 505/466–4008, *www.galisteoinn.com*. 12 rooms. *Restaurant, pool, hot tub, sauna; no kids under 10, no smoking. D, MC, V. BP.*

El Rancho de las Golondrinas

30 *15 mi south of Santa Fe off I–25's Exit 276 in La Cienega.*

The "Williamsburg of the Southwest," El Rancho de las Golondrinas ("the ranch of the swallows") is a reconstruction of a small agricultural village. Originally a *paraje*, or stopping place, on El Camino Real, the village has buildings from the

17th to 19th century. By car, the ranch is only a 25-minute drive from the Plaza. From Interstate 25, the village is tucked away from view, frozen in time. Owned and operated by the Paloheimo family, direct descendants of those who owned the ranch when it functioned as a paraje, the restored grounds of this living museum maintain an authentic character without compromising history for commercial gain. Guided tours (April–October) survey Spanish-colonial lifestyles in New Mexico from 1660 to 1890: you can view a molasses mill, threshing grounds, and wheelwright and blacksmith shops, as well as a mountain village and a *morada* (meeting place) of the order of Penitentes (a religious fraternity known for its reenactment during Holy Week of the tortures suffered by Christ). Farm animals roam through the barnyards on the 200-acre complex. Wool from the sheep is spun into yarn and woven into traditional Rio Grande–style blankets, and the corn grown is dried and used to feed the animals. During the spring and harvest festivals, on the first weekends of June and October, respectively, the village comes alive with Spanish-American folk music, dancing, and food and crafts demonstrations. *334 Los Pinos Rd., tel. 505/471–2261, www.golondrinas.org. $5. Wed.–Sun. 10–4.*

GEORGIA O'KEEFFE COUNTRY

It's just a 20-minute drive north of Santa Fe to reach the Española Valley, which leads to the striking mesas, cliffs, and valleys that so inspired the artist Georgia O'Keeffe—she lived in this area for the final 50 years of her life. You'll first come to the small, workaday city of Española, a major crossroads from which roads lead to Taos, Chama, and Abiquiu. The other notable community in this area is tiny Ojo Caliente, famous for its hot-springs spa retreat.

Española

31 *20 mi north of Santa Fe via U.S. 285/84.*

This small but growing city midway along the Low Road from Santa Fe to Taos is a little rough around the edges—it was founded in the 1880s as a stop on the Denver and Rio Grande Railroad, and it lacks the colonial charm of either Santa Fe or Taos. Española is rather busy today and has many cheap restaurants, a few chain motels, but few reasons to stick around for more than a quick meal. One of the city's modern trademarks is lowriders, which you'll see cruising the streets. They're mostly classic cars that have been retrofitted with lowered chassis and hydraulics that often allow the cars to bump and grind; the cars are often painted with spectacular murals, from religious art to scenes of the region's landscape.

All of the main arteries converge in the heart of town in a confusing, unpleasant maze of drab shopping centers, so watch the signs on the south side of town. Traffic moves slowly, especially on weekend nights when cruisers bring car culture alive.

WHERE TO EAT AND STAY

$–$$ EL PARAGUA RESTAURANT. ★ With a dark, intimate atmosphere of wood and stone, this historic place started out as a lemonade–cum–taco stand in the late 1950s but is now known for some of the state's most authentic New Mexican and regional Mexican cuisine. Steaks and fish are grilled over a mesquite-wood fire; other specialties include chorizo enchiladas, panfried breaded trout Amadine, and menudo. *603 Santa Cruz Rd. (NM 76 just east of NM 68), tel. 505/753–3211 or 800/929–8226. AE, DC, MC, V.*

$$$–$$$$ RANCHO DE SAN JUAN. ★ Well north of Española's bustle and a great choice if you're visiting Abiquiu or Ojo Caliente, this secluded 225-acre Relaix & Châteaux compound hugs the base of Black Mesa. Many of the rooms at the understated and very romantic inn are self-contained suites, some set around a central courtyard and others farther out amid the wilderness. All rooms have museum-quality southwestern furnishings, CD stereos, and local artwork; some rooms have fireplaces, Jacuzzi tubs, and full kitchens. A four-course prix-fixe dinner of some of New Mexico's finest contemporary cooking is available (by reservation only) in the intimate restaurant ($$$$), Wednesday through Sunday. Guests can hike up to a serene hand-carved sandstone shrine on a bluff high above the property. Spa and massage services are also available. U.S. 285, 3½ mi north of U.S. 84 (Box 4140, Española 87533), tel. 505/753–6818 or 800/726–7121, www.ranchodesanjuan.com. 9 rooms, 8 suites. Restaurant, some kitchens, hiking. AE, D, DC, MC, V.

Abiquiu

32 24 mi northwest of Española via U.S. 84.

This tiny, very traditional Hispanic village was home to genizaros, people of mixed tribal backgrounds with Spanish surnames. The surnames came from Spanish families who used Indians as servants. Many descendants of original families still live in the area, although since the late 1980s Abiquiu and its surrounding countryside have become a nesting ground for those fleeing big-city lifestyles, among them actresses Marsha Mason and Shirley MacLaine. A feeling of insider versus outsider and old-timer versus newcomer still prevails. Newcomers or visitors may find themselves resented; it's best to observe one very important local custom: no photography is allowed in and around the village.

You can visit **GEORGIA O'KEEFFE'S HOME** through advance reservation (four months recommended) with the **Georgia O'Keeffe Foundation** (tel. 505/685–4359, www.abiquiuinn.com/tour.html), which conducts one-hour tours Tuesday, Thursday, and Friday, April–November, for $22. In 1945 Georgia O'Keeffe bought a large, dilapidated late-18th-century Spanish-colonial adobe compound just off the Plaza. Upon the 1946 death of her husband, photographer Alfred Stieglitz, she left New York City and began dividing her time permanently between this home, which figured prominently in many of her works, and the one in nearby Ghost Ranch. She wrote about the house, "When I first saw the Abiquiú house it was a ruin . . . As I climbed and walked about in the ruin I found a patio with a very pretty well house and a bucket to draw up water. It was a good-sized patio with a long wall with a door on one side. That wall with a door in it was something I had to have. It took me 10 years to get it—three more years to fix the house up so I could live in it—and after that the wall with the door was painted many times." The patio is featured in *Black Patio Door* (1955) and *Patio with Cloud* (1956). O'Keeffe died in 1986 at the age of 98 and left provisions in her will to ensure that the property's houses would never be public monuments.

WHERE TO EAT AND STAY

$–$$ **ABIQUIU INN AND CAFE ABIQUIU.** Deep in the Chama Valley, the inn has a secluded, exotic feel—almost like an oasis—with lavishly decorated rooms, including several four-person casitas, with woodstoves or fireplaces and tiled baths. Middle Eastern and Mediterranean cuisine is on the menu at the café ($–$$). The inn is owned and operated by the Dar al-Islam mosque and is the departure point for tours of the O'Keeffe home. It has an exceptional art gallery, crafts shop, and gardens. *U.S. 84 (Box 120, Abiquiu 87510), tel. 505/685–4378 or 800/447–5621, fax 800/447–5621 ext. *2, www.abiquiuinn.com. 19 rooms, 5 casitas. Restaurant, shops. AE, D, DC, MC, V.*

Ghost Ranch

③③ *10 mi northwest of Abiquiu on U.S. 84.*

For art historians, the name Ghost Ranch brings to mind Georgia O'Keeffe, who lived on but a small parcel of this 20,000-acre dude and cattle ranch. The ranch's owner in the 1930s—conservationist and publisher of *Nature Magazine* Arthur Pack—first invited O'Keeffe here to visit in 1934; Pack soon sold the artist the 7-acre plot on which she lived summer through fall for most of the rest of her life.

In 1955, Pack donated the rest of the ranch to the Presbyterian Church, which continues to use Pack's original structures and about 55 acres of land as a conference center.

The **GHOST RANCH CONFERENCE CENTER** (U.S. 84, tel. 505/685–4333 or 800/821–5145, plazaresolana.org), open year-round, is busiest in summer, when dozens of workshops take place. Subjects range from poetry and literary arts to photography, horseback riding, and every conceivable traditional craft of northern New Mexico. Guests camp or stay in semi-rustic cottages or casitas. After registering at the main office, you may come in and hike high among the wind-hewn rocks so beloved by O'Keeffe (but her original house is closed to the public).

Ojo Caliente

34 *28 mi northeast of Abiquiu by way of El Rito via NM 554 to NM 111 to U.S. 285; 50 mi north of Santa Fe on U.S. 285.*

Ojo Caliente is the only place in North America where five different types of hot springs—iron, lithia, arsenic, salt, and soda—are found side by side. The town was named by Spanish explorer Cabeza de Vaca, who visited in 1535 and believed he had stumbled upon the Fountain of Youth.

WHERE TO STAY

$$–$$$ **OJO CALIENTE MINERAL SPRINGS SPA AND RESORT.** Accommodations at this spa are decidedly spartan, with down comforters on the beds and rudimentary bathrooms without showers or tubs—you've come for the mineral springs, after all, and that's where the bathing takes place. Lodgers have complimentary access to the mineral pools and milagro (miracle) wraps, and the bathhouse is equipped with showers. Some cottages have kitchenettes. Horseback tours of the area must be prearranged,

so notify the office in advance. Poppy's Cafe serves New Mexican specialties. *50 Los Baños Dr. (Box 68, 87549), off U.S. 285, 30 mi north of Española, tel. 505/583–2233 or 800/222–9162, fax 505/583–2464, www.ojocalientespa.com. 19 rooms, 19 cottages, 2 3-bedroom houses. Restaurant, some kitchenettes, some refrigerators, massage, spa, meeting rooms; no room phones, no TV in some rooms. AE, D, DC, MC, V.*

THE HIGH ROAD TO TAOS

The main highway to Taos along the Rio Grande gorge (NM 68) provides dramatic close-ups of the river and rocky mountain faces (☞ Low Road to Santa Fe in Side Trips in Chapter 5), but if you have an extra hour or two, the High Road to Taos is worth choosing for its views of sweeping woodlands and traditional Hispanic villages. The High Road follows U.S. 285 north to NM 503 (a right turn just past Pojoaque), to County Road 98 (a left toward Chimayó), to NM 76 northeast to NM 75 east, to NM 518 north. The drive through the rolling foothills and tiny valleys of the Sangre de Cristos, dotted with orchards, pueblos, and picturesque villages, is stunning. In mid-April the orchards are in blossom; summer turns the valleys into lush green oases; and in fall, the smell of piñon adds to the sensual overload of golden leaves and red-chile ristras hanging from the houses. In winter, the fields are covered with quilts of snow, and the lines of homes, fences, and trees stand out like bold pen-and-ink drawings against the sky. But the roads can be icy and treacherous—if in doubt, stick with the "low road" to Taos. If you decide to take the High Road just one way between Santa Fe and Taos, you might want to save it for the return journey—the scenery is best enjoyed when traveling north to south.

Chimayó

35 28 mi north of Santa Fe, 10 mi east of Española on NM 76.

From U.S. 285/84 north of Pojoaque, scenic NM 503 winds past horse paddocks and orchards in the narrow Nambé Valley, then ascends into the red-sandstone canyons with a view of Truchas Peaks to the northeast before dropping into the bucolic village of Chimayó. Nestled into hillsides where gnarled piñons seem to grow from bare bedrock, Chimayó is famed for its weaving, its red chiles, and its two chapels.

The **SANTUARIO DE CHIMAYÓ**, a small frontier adobe church, has a fantastically carved and painted wood altar and is built on the site where, believers say, a mysterious light came from the ground on Good Friday in 1810 and where a large wooden crucifix was found beneath the earth. The chapel sits above a sacred *pozito* (a small hole), the dirt from which is believed to have miraculous healing properties. Dozens of abandoned crutches and braces placed in the anteroom—along with many notes, letters, and photos—testify to this. The Santuario draws a steady stream of worshipers all year long—Chimayó is considered the Lourdes of the Southwest. During Holy Week as many as 50,000 pilgrims come here. The shrine is a National Historic Landmark. It's also surrounded by commercialism in the way of small adobe shops selling every kind of religious curio imaginable. Mass is celebrated on Sunday. *Signed lane off C.R. 98, tel. 505/351–4889. Free. Daily 9–5.*

A smaller chapel just 200 yards from El Santuario was built in 1857 and dedicated to **SANTO NIÑO DE ATOCHA.** As at the more famous Santuario, the dirt at Santo Niño de Atocha's chapel is said to have healing properties in the place where the *Santo Niño* was first placed. The little boy saint was brought here from Mexico by Severiano Medina, who claimed Santo Niño de Atocha had healed him of rheumatism. San Ildefonso pottery master Maria Martinez came here for healing as a child. Tales of the boy saint's losing one of his shoes as he wandered through the countryside helping those in trouble endeared him to the people of northern New Mexico. It became a tradition to place shoes at the foot of the statue as an offering. *Free. Daily 9–5.*

WHERE TO EAT AND STAY

$$ RANCHO DE CHIMAYÓ. In a century-old adobe hacienda tucked into the mountains, with whitewashed walls, hand-stripped vigas, and cozy dining rooms, the much-hyped Rancho de Chimayó is still owned and operated by the family that first occupied the house. There's a roaring fireplace in winter and, in summer, a terraced patio shaded by catalpa trees. Good, if predictable, New Mexican fare is served, but the ambience is the real draw here. You can take an after-dinner stroll on the grounds' paths. Reservations are essential in summer. *C.R. 98, tel. 505/351–4444. AE, D, DC, MC, V. Closed Mon. Nov.–mid-May.*

$–$$ CASA ESCONDIDA. Intimate and peaceful, this adobe inn has sweeping views of the Sangre de Cristo range. The setting makes it a great base for mountain bikers. Chopin on the CD player and the scent of fresh-baked strudel waft through the rooms. Rooms are decorated with antiques and Native American and other regional arts and crafts. Ask for the Sun Room, in the main house, which has a private patio, viga ceilings, and a brick floor. The separate one-bedroom Casita Escondida has a kiva-style fireplace, tile floors, kitchenette, and a sitting area. A large hot tub is hidden in a grove behind wild berry bushes. *Off NM 76 at C.R. 0100 (Box 142, 85722), tel. 505/351–4805 or 800/643–7201, fax 505/351–2575, www.casaescondida.com. 7 rooms, 1 house. Some kitchenettes, outdoor hot tub. MC, V. BP.*

$–$$ HACIENDA DE CHIMAYÓ. This authentic adobe house is furnished with antiques, and each room has a private bath and fireplace. The inn sits directly on Chimayó's main road and is conveniently across from the lovely Rancho de Chimayó restaurant and within walking distance of the Santuario. *C.R. 98 (Box 11, Chimayó 87522), tel. 505/351–2222, www.ranchodechimayo.com. 6 rooms, 1 suite. AE, D, DC, MC, V. CP.*

SHOPPING

CENTINELA TRADITIONAL ARTS-WEAVING (NM 76, 1 mi east of junction with C.R. 98, tel. 505/351–2180 or 877/351–2180) continues the Trujillo family weaving tradition, which started in northern New Mexico more than seven generations ago. Irvin Trujillo and his wife, Lisa, are both award-winning master weavers, creating Rio Grande–style tapestry blankets and rugs, many of them with natural dyes that authentically replicate early weavings. Most designs are historically based, but the Trujillos contribute their own designs as well. The shop and gallery carries these heirloom-quality textiles, with a knowledgeable staff on hand to demonstrate or answer questions about the weaving technique.

ORTEGA'S WEAVING SHOP (NM 76 at C.R. 98, tel. 505/351–4215 or 877/351–4215) sells Rio Grande– and Chimayó-style textiles made by the family whose Spanish ancestors brought the craft to New Mexico in the 1600s. The Galeria Ortega, next door, sells traditional New Mexican and Hispanic and contemporary Native American arts and crafts. The shop is closed on Sunday.

Cordova

🐧 *4 mi east of Chimayó via NM 76.*

A minuscule mountain village with a small central plaza, a school, a post office, and a church, Cordova is the center of the regional wood-carving industry. The town supports more than 30 full-time and part-time carvers. Most of them are descendants of José Dolores López, who in the 1920s created the village's signature unpainted "Cordova style" of carving. Most of the *santeros* (makers of religious images) have signs outside their homes indicating that santos are for sale. The pieces are expensive, ranging from several hundred dollars for small ones to several thousand for larger figures. There are also affordable and delightful small carvings of animals and birds. The St. Anthony of Padua Chapel, which is filled with handcrafted retablos and other religious art, is worth a visit.

Eating Well Is the Best Revenge

Eating out is a major part of every travel experience. It's a chance to explore flavors you don't find at home. And often the walking you do on vacation means that you can dig in without guilt.

START AT THE TOP By all means take in a really good restaurant or two while you're on the road. A trip is a time to kick back and savor the pleasures of the palate. Read up on the culinary scene before you leave home. Check out representative menus on the Web—some chefs have gone electronic. And ask friends who have just come back. Then reserve a table as far in advance as you can, remembering that the best establishments book up months in advance. Remember that some good restaurants require you to reconfirm the day before or the day of your meal. Then again, some really good places will call you, so make sure to leave a number where you can be reached.

ADVENTURES IN EATING A trip is the perfect opportunity to try food you can't get at home. So leave yourself open to try an ethnic food that's not represented where you live or to eat fruits and vegetables you've never heard of. One of them may become your next favorite food.

BEYOND GUIDEBOOKS You can rely on the restaurants you find in these pages. But also look for restaurants on your own. When you're ready for lunch, ask people you meet where they eat. Look for tiny holes-in-the-wall with a loyal following and the best burgers or crispiest pizza crust. Find out about local chains whose fame rests upon a single memorable dish. There's hardly a food-lover who doesn't relish the chance to share a favorite place. It's fun to come up with your own special find—and asking about food is a great way to start a conversation.

SAMPLE LOCAL FLAVORS Do check out the specialties. Is there a special brand of ice cream or a special dish that you simply must try?

HAVE A PICNIC Every so often eat al fresco. Grocery shopping gives you a whole different view of a place.

Truchas

⊙ 4 mi northeast of Cordova via NM 76.

Truchas (Spanish for "trout") is where Robert Redford shot the movie *The Milagro Beanfield War* (based on the much better novel written by Taos author John Nichols). This village is perched on the rim of a deep canyon beneath the towering Truchas Peaks, mountains high enough to be almost perpetually capped with snow. The tallest of the Truchas Peaks is 13,102 ft, the second-highest point in New Mexico. There are a few galleries and a small market in this town, which feels like an outpost just waking up from the colonial days. Continue 7 mi north on NM 76, toward Taos, and you'll come to the marvelous San Tomás Church in the village of Trampas. It dates from at least 1760.

SHOPPING
The most notable of the colorful shops and galleries in Truchas is **CORDOVAS HANDWEAVING WORKSHOP** (village center, tel. 505/689–2437).

In This Chapter

Updated by Holly Hammond

taos

TAOS CASTS A LINGERING SPELL. Majestic Taos Mountain presides over the valley, where the air smells of piñon smoke and sagebrush. The two-centuries-old Plaza and old adobe buildings testify to the town's Native American and Spanish origins. Many roads and lanes around town remain unpaved and rutted, and vacation homes take their place among farmsteads handed down from Spanish-colonial days.

With a population of about 6,500, Taos, on a rolling mesa at the base of the Sangre de Cristo Mountains, is actually three towns in one. The first is the low-key business district of art galleries, restaurants, and shops that recalls the Santa Fe of a few decades ago. The second area, 3 mi north of the commercial center, is Taos Pueblo, home to Tiwa-speaking Native Americans. Life at the Taos Pueblo long predates the arrival of the Spanish in America in the 1500s. Unlike many nomadic Native American tribes that were forced to relocate to government-designated reservations, the residents of Taos Pueblo have inhabited their land (at present 95,000 acres) at the base of the 12,282-ft-high Taos Mountain for centuries.

The third part of Taos, 4 mi south of town, is Ranchos de Taos, a farming and ranching community settled by the Spanish. Ranchos is best known for the San Francisco de Asís Church, whose buttressed adobe walls shelter significant religious artifacts and paintings. Its massive exterior and *camposanto* (graveyard) are among the most photographed in the country.

That so many 20th-century painters, photographers, and literary figures—among them Georgia O'Keeffe, Ansel Adams, and D. H. Lawrence—have been drawn to the earthy spirit of Taos has only heightened its appeal. Bert Phillips and Ernest Blumenschein, traveling from Denver on a planned painting trip into Mexico in 1898, stopped in Taos to have a broken wagon wheel repaired. Enthralled with the landscape, earth-hue adobe buildings, piercing light, and clean mountain air, they abandoned their plan to journey farther south. They returned to the Taos area often, speaking so highly of it that other East Coast artists followed them west. By 1915, the Taos Society of Artists had been established. Blumenschein and Phillips, with Joseph Henry Sharp and Eanger Irving Couse, all graduates of the Paris art school Académie Julian, formed the core of the group.

The persuasive hospitality of transplanted socialite Mabel Dodge Luhan also drew cultural luminaries here. Some of the early Taos artists spent their winters in New York or Chicago teaching painting or illustration to earn enough money to summer in New Mexico. Others became full-time New Mexicans. Living conditions were primitive then: no running water, electricity, or even indoor plumbing. But these painters happily endured such inconveniences to indulge their fascination with Native American customs, modes of dress, and ceremonies. Eventually, they co-opted the Native architecture and dress and presumptuously fancied that they "knew" Indian culture. The Society of Artists disbanded in 1927, but Taos continued to attract artists. Several galleries opened and, in 1952, local painters joined together to form the Taos Artists' Association, forerunner to today's Taos Art Association. At present, several dozen galleries and shops display art, sculpture, and crafts, and about 1,000 artists live in town or nearby. No mere satellite of Santa Fe, Taos is an art center in its own right.

HERE AND THERE

Taos is small and resolutely rustic, and the central area is highly walkable. Sociable Taoseños make the town a welcoming place to explore. You'll need a car to reach the Enchanted Circle, the Rio Grande Gorge, Taos Ski Valley, and other places of interest beyond Taos proper. Traffic can be heavy in the peak summer and winter seasons; ask locals about back roads that let you avoid the busy Paseo del Pueblo.

The Museum Association of Taos includes seven properties. Among them are the Harwood Museum, the Fechin Institute, the Millicent Rogers Museum, and the Van Vechten–Lineberry Taos Art Museum, as well as those in the Kit Carson Historic Museum consortium: the Blumenschein Home and Museum, the Kit Carson Home and Museum, and La Hacienda de los Martínez. Each of the museums charges $4 or $5 for admission, but you can opt for a combination ticket—$20 for all seven, valid for one year, or buy a $10 joint ticket to the three Kit Carson museums.

Numbers in the text correspond to numbers in the margin and on the Taos map.

DOWNTOWN TAOS

More than four centuries after it was laid out, Taos Plaza remains the center of commercial life in Taos. Bent Street, where New Mexico's first American governor lived and died, is an upscale shopping area and gallery enclave.

What to See

② BLUMENSCHEIN HOME AND MUSEUM. For an introduction to the history of the Taos art scene, start with Ernest L. Blumenschein's residence, which provides a glimpse into the cosmopolitan lives led by the members of the Taos Society of Artists, of which Blumenschein was a founding member. One of the rooms in the

taos

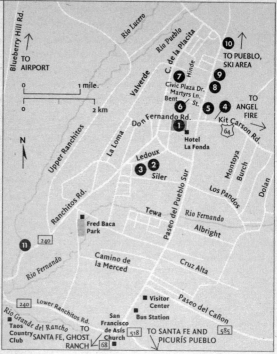

adobe-style structure dates from 1797. On display are the art, antiques, and other personal possessions of Blumenschein and his wife, Mary Greene Blumenschein, who also painted, as did their daughter Helen. Several of Ernest Blumenschein's vivid oil paintings hang in his former studio, and also on display are works by other early Taos artists. *222 Ledoux St., tel. 505/758-0505. $5 (or use Kit Carson Historic Museums of Taos joint ticket). Apr.–Oct., daily 9–5; Nov.–Mar., daily 10–4.*

★ ❾ **FECHIN INSTITUTE.** The interior of this extraordinary adobe house, built between 1927 and 1933 by Russian émigré and artist Nicolai Fechin, is a marvel of carved Russian-style woodwork and furniture that glistens with an almost golden sheen. Fechin constructed it to showcase his daringly colorful paintings. Fechin's daughter Eya oversees her father's architectural masterpiece—she loves talking about him and life "back then" (she arrived in Taos with her father when she was 12). Listed on the National Register of Historic Places, the Fechin Institute hosts exhibits and special workshops devoted to the artist's unique approach to learning, teaching, and creating. Open hours are often in flux, so call ahead. *227 Paseo del Pueblo Norte, tel. 505/758–1710. $4. Wed.–Sun. 10–2.*

Ⓒ ❼ **FIREHOUSE COLLECTION.** More than 100 works by well-known Taos artists like Joseph Sharp, Ernest L. Blumenschein, and Bert Phillips hang in the Taos Volunteer Fire Department building. The exhibition space adjoins the station house, where five fire engines are maintained at the ready and an antique fire engine is on display. *321 Camino de la Placita, tel. 505/758–3386. Free. Weekdays 9–4:30.*

Ⓒ ❻ **GOVERNOR BENT MUSEUM.** In 1846, when New Mexico became a U.S. possession as a result of the Mexican War, Charles Bent, a trader, trapper, and mountain man, was appointed governor. Less than a year later he was killed in his house by an angry mob protesting New Mexico's annexation by the United States. Governor Bent was married to María Ignacia, the older sister of

Josefa Jaramillo, the wife of mountain man Kit Carson. A collection of Native American artifacts, western Americana, and family possessions is squeezed into five small rooms of the adobe building where Bent and his family lived. *117 Bent St., tel. 505/758–2376. $1. Daily 10–5.*

★ ❸ **HARWOOD FOUNDATION.** The Pueblo Revival former home of Burritt Elihu "Burt" Harwood, a dedicated painter who studied in France before moving to Taos with his public-spirited wife, Lucy, in 1916, is adjacent to a museum dedicated to the works of local artists. Traditional Hispanic northern New Mexican artists, early art-colony painters, post–World War II Modernists, and contemporary artists such as Larry Bell, Agnes Martin, Ken Price, and Earl Stroh are represented. Mabel Dodge Luhan, a major arts patron, bequeathed many of the 19th-century and early 20th-century works in the Harwoods' collection, including *retablos* (painted wood representations of Catholic saints) and *bultos* (three-dimensional carvings of the saints). In the Hispanic Traditions Gallery upstairs are 19th-century tinwork, furniture, and sculpture. Downstairs, among early 20th-century art-colony holdings, look for E. Martin Hennings's *Chamisa in Bloom*. A tour of the ground-floor galleries shows that Taos painters of the era, notably Oscar Berninghaus, Ernest Blumenschein, Victor Higgins, Walter Ufer, Marsden Hartley, and John Marin, were fascinated by the land and the people linked to it. An octagonal gallery exhibits works by Agnes Martin. Martin's seven large canvas panels (5 ft by 5 ft) are studies in white, their precise lines and blocks forming textured grids. Operated by the University of New Mexico since 1936, the Harwood is the second-oldest art museum in the state. *238 Ledoux St., tel. 505/758–9826. $5. Tues.–Sat. 10–5, Sun. noon–5.*

🖐 ❹ **KIT CARSON HOME AND MUSEUM.** Kit Carson bought this low-slung 12-room adobe home in 1843 for his wife, Josefa Jaramillo, the daughter of a powerful, politically influential Spanish family. Three of the museum's rooms are furnished as they were when the Carson family lived here. The rest of the museum is devoted to gun and mountain-man exhibits, such as rugged leather clothing and Kit's own Spencer carbine rifle with its beaded leather carrying case, and early Taos antiques, artifacts, and manuscripts. *Kit Carson Rd., tel. 505/758–0505. $5 (or use Kit Carson Historic Museums of Taos joint ticket). Apr.–Oct., daily 9–5; call for winter hrs.*

NEED A BREAK? Let the coffee aroma draw you into the tiny **WORLD CUP** (102 Paseo del Pueblo Norte, tel. 505/737–5299).

⑧ KIT CARSON MEMORIAL PARK. The noted pioneer is buried in the park that bears his name. His grave is marked with a *cerquita* (a spiked wrought-iron rectangular fence), traditionally used to outline and protect burial sites. Also interred here is Mabel Dodge Luhan, the pioneering patron of the early Taos art scene. The 20-acre park has swings and slides for recreational breaks. It's well marked with big stone pillars and a gate. *Paseo del Pueblo Norte at Civic Plaza Dr., tel. 505/758–8234. Free. Late May–early Sept., daily 8–8; early Sept.–late May, daily 8–5.*

⑤ STABLES ART CENTER. It was in the stables in back of this house that the Taos Artists' Association first began showing the works of members and invited nonmember artists from across northern New Mexico. In 1952 the association purchased the handsome adobe building, which is now the visual arts gallery of the Taos Art Association. All the work on exhibit is for sale. *133 Paseo del Pueblo Norte, tel. 505/758–2036. Free. Daily 10–5.*

① TAOS PLAZA. The first European explorers of the Taos Valley came here with Captain Hernando de Alvarado, a member of Francisco Vásquez de Coronado's expedition of 1540. Basque explorer Don Juan de Oñate arrived in Taos in July 1598 and established a mission and trading arrangements with residents of Taos Pueblo. The settlement developed into two plazas: the Plaza at the heart of the town became a thriving business district for the early colony, and a walled residential plaza was constructed a few hundred yards behind. It remains active today, home to a throng of gift and coffee shops. The covered gazebo was donated by heiress and longtime Taos resident Mabel Dodge Luhan. On the southeastern corner of Taos Plaza is the **Hotel La Fonda de Taos.** Some infamous erotic paintings by D. H. Lawrence that were naughty in his day but are quite tame by present standards can be viewed ($2 entry fee) in the former barroom beyond the lobby.

NEED A BREAK? To fuel your walk, grab a pick-me-up at **TRANS-FU'SION** (204 Paseo del Pueblo Norte, tel. 505/758–5842), a coffee bar that serves smoothies and an array of herbal tonic drinks as well as java.

⑩ VAN VECHTEN–LINEBERRY TAOS ART MUSEUM. This privately run museum shows the works of painter Duane Van Vechten, the late wife of Edwin C. Lineberry. Her former studio is the entrance to the museum, whose collection of 130 works by more than 50 Taos artists includes pieces of varying quality by the founders of the Taos Society of Artists. The museum's signature piece is *Our Lady of Gualadupe* (1929) by Van Vechten. On a par with the exhibits are the museum grounds, a 10-acre walled park, and the building itself, which was the home of the artist and Mr. Lineberry, who maintains the museum with his wife, Novella. *501 Paseo del Pueblo Norte, tel. 505/758–2690. $6. Wed.–Fri. 10–5, Sat. 1–5, Sun. 1–4.*

NEED A BREAK? Join the locals at the north or south location of the **BEAN** (900 Paseo del Pueblo Norte, tel. 505/758–7111; 1033 Paseo del Pueblo Sur, tel. 505/758–5123). The Bean roasts its own coffee, and the south-side location offers breakfast and lunch.

SOUTH OF TAOS

The first Spanish settlers were farmers who faced raids by non–Pueblo Indians like the Comanches. Aspects of this history come alive on this meandering drive south through fields and farmland to a restored hacienda and into a former farming village with its famous, fortresslike church.

What to See

⑪ **LA HACIENDA DE LOS MARTÍNEZ.** Spare and fortlike, this adobe structure built between 1804 and 1827 on the bank of the Rio Pueblo served as a community refuge during Comanche and Apache raids. Its thick walls, which have few windows, surround two central courtyards. Don Antonio Severino Martínez was a farmer and trader; the hacienda was the final stop along El Camino Real (the Royal Road), the trade route the Spanish established between Mexico City and New Mexico. The restored period rooms here contain textiles, foods, and crafts of the early 19th century. There's a working blacksmith's shop, and weavers create beautiful textiles on reconstructed period looms. During the last weekend in September the hacienda hosts the Old Taos Trade Fair. *Ranchitos Rd.* (NM 240), *tel.* 505/758-0505. *$5 (or use Kit Carson Historic Museums of Taos joint ticket). Apr.–Oct., daily 9–5; Nov.–Mar., daily 10–4.*

OFF THE BEATEN PATH **PICURÍS PUEBLO** – The Picurís (Keresan for "those who paint") Native Americans once lived in six- and seven-story dwellings similar to those still standing at the Taos Pueblo, but these were abandoned in the wake of 18th-century Pueblo uprisings. Relatively isolated about 30 mi south of Taos, Picurís, one of the smallest pueblos in New Mexico, is surrounded by the timberland of the Carson National Forest. The 270-member Tiwa-speaking Picurís tribe is a sovereign nation and has no treaties with any country, including the United States. You can tour the village and 700-year-old ruins of kivas (ceremonial rooms) and storage areas, which were excavated in 1961. The exhibits in the pueblo's museum include pottery and some ruins. The Hidden Valley Restaurant also has a gift shop. Fishing, picnicking, and camping are allowed at nearby trout-stocked Pu-Na and Tu-Tah lakes. Fishing and camping permits can be obtained at the restaurant (no state fishing license is required). The pueblo honors its patron saint, San Lorenzo, with a festival on August 9 and 10. An example of the Picurís people's enterprising spirit is their majority interest in the lovely Hotel Santa Fe in the state's capital city; many pueblo members commute to work there. *NM 75, Peñasco (from Ranchos de Taos head south on NM 518, east on NM 75, and turn right at signs for village; from NM 68 head east on NM 75 and make a left into village), tel. 505/587–2519, www.picurispueblo.com. Museum free, self-guided walking or driving tour $1.75, still-camera permit $5 (includes $1.75 fee for camera holder), video camera or sketching permit $10 (includes $1.75 tour fee). Daily 8–5, but call ahead especially early Sept.–late May, when the pueblo is sometimes closed.*

⑫ **RANCHOS DE TAOS.** A few minutes' drive south of the center of Taos, this village still retains some of its rural atmosphere despite the highway traffic passing through. Huddled around its famous adobe church and dusty plaza are cheerful, remodeled shops and galleries standing shoulder to shoulder with crumbling adobe shells. This ranching, farming, and budding small-business community was an early home to Taos Native Americans before being settled by Spaniards in 1716. While many of the adobe dwellings have seen better days, the shops, modest galleries, taco stands, and two fine restaurants point to an ongoing revival.

The massive bulk of **San Francisco de Asís Church** (*NM 68, 500 yards south of NM 518, Ranchos de Taos, tel. 505/758–2754*) is an enduring attraction. The Spanish Mission–style church was erected in 1815 as a spiritual and physical refuge from raiding Apaches, Utes, and Comanches. In 1979 the deteriorated church was rebuilt with traditional adobe bricks by community volunteers. Every spring a group gathers to re-mud the facade. The earthy, clean lines of the exterior walls and supporting bulwarks have inspired generations of painters and photographers. The late-afternoon light provides the best exposure of the heavily buttressed rear of the church—though today's image-takers face the challenge of framing the architecturally pure lines through rows of parked cars and a large, white sign put up by church officials; morning light is best for the front. Bells in the twin belfries call Taoseños to services on Sunday and holidays. From Monday through Saturday from 9 to 4 you can step inside. In the parish hall nearby a 15-minute video presentation every half hour describes the history and restoration of the church and explains the mysterious painting, *Shadow of the Cross*, on which each evening the shadow of a cross appears over Christ's shoulder. Scientific studies made on the canvas and the paint pigments cannot explain the phenomenon. *Paseo del Pueblo Sur (NM 68), about 4 mi south of Taos Plaza.*

NEED A BREAK? The storefront **RANCHOS COFFEE COMPANY** (1574 Paseo del Pueblo Sur, tel. 505/751–0653) has fresh coffee, tea, pastries, and sandwiches.

TAOS PUEBLO TO RIO GRANDE GORGE

What to See

⑭ **MILLICENT ROGERS MUSEUM.** More than 5,000 pieces of Native American and Hispanic art, the core of Standard Oil heiress Millicent Rogers's private collection, are on exhibit here: baskets, blankets, rugs, jewelry, katsina dolls, carvings, paintings, and rare religious and secular artifacts. Of major importance are the pottery and ceramics of Maria Martinez and other potters from San Ildefonso Pueblo. Docents conduct guided tours by appointment, and the museum hosts lectures, films, workshops, and demonstrations. *1504 Millicent Rogers Rd. (from Taos Plaza head north on Paseo del Pueblo Norte and left at the sign for C.R. BA030—also called Millicent Rogers Rd. or Museum Rd.), tel. 505/758–2462, www.millicentrogers.com. $6. Apr.–Sept., daily 10–5; Nov.–Mar., Tues.–Sun. 10–5.*

☝ ❶⑮ **RIO GRANDE GORGE BRIDGE.** It's a breathtaking experience to see the Rio Grande flowing 650 ft underfoot. The bridge is the second-highest expansion bridge in the country. Hold on to your camera and eyeglasses when looking down, and watch out for low-flying planes. The Taos Municipal Airport is close by, and daredevil private pilots have been known to challenge one another to fly under the bridge. Shortly after daybreak, hot air balloons fly above and even inside the gorge. *U.S. 64, 12 mi west of town.*

★ ☝ ⑬ **TAOS PUEBLO.** For nearly 1,000 years the mud-and-straw adobe walls of Taos Pueblo have sheltered Tiwa-speaking Native Americans. A United Nations World Heritage Site, this is the largest multistory pueblo structure in the United States. The two main buildings, Hlauuma (north house) and Hlaukwima (south house), separated by a creek, are believed to be of a similar age, probably constructed between 1000 and 1450. The dwellings have common walls but no connecting doorways—the Tiwas gained access only from the top, via ladders that were retrieved after entering. Small buildings and corrals are scattered about.

The pueblo today appears much as it did when the first Spanish explorers arrived in New Mexico in 1540. The adobe walls glistening with mica caused the conquistadors to believe they had discovered one of the fabled Seven Cities of Gold. The outside surfaces are continuously maintained by replastering with thin layers of mud, and the interior walls are frequently coated with thin washes of white clay. Some walls are several feet thick in places. The roofs of each of the five-story structures are supported by large timbers, or *vigas*, hauled down from the mountain forests. Pine or aspen *latillas* (smaller pieces of wood) are placed side by side between the vigas; the entire roof is then packed with dirt.

Even after 400 years of Spanish and Anglo presence in Taos, inside the pueblo the traditional Native American way of life has endured. Tribal custom allows no electricity or running water in Hlauuma and Hlaukwima, where varying numbers (usually fewer than 100) of Taos Native Americans live full-time. About 2,000 others live in conventional homes on the pueblo's 95,000 acres. The crystal-clear Rio Pueblo de Taos, originating high above in the mountains at the sacred Blue Lake, is the primary source of water for drinking and irrigating. Bread is still baked in *hornos* (outdoor domed ovens). Artisans of the Taos Pueblo produce and sell (tax-free) traditionally handcrafted wares, such as mica-flecked pottery and silver jewelry. Great hunters, the Taos Native Americans are also known for their work with animal skins and their excellent moccasins, boots, and drums.

Although the population is about 80% Catholic, the people of Taos Pueblo, like most Pueblo Native Americans, also maintain their native religious traditions. At Christmas and other sacred holidays, for instance, immediately after Mass, dancers dressed in seasonal sacred garb proceed down the aisle of St. Jerome Chapel, drums beating and rattles shaking, to begin other religious rites.

The pueblo **Church of San Geronimo**, or St. Jerome, the patron saint of Taos Pueblo, was completed in 1850 to replace the one destroyed by the U.S. Army in 1847 during the Mexican War. With its smooth symmetry, stepped portal, and twin bell towers, the church is a popular subject for photographers and artists (though the taking of photographs inside is discouraged).

The public is invited to certain ceremonial dances held throughout the year: January 1, Turtle Dance; January 6, Buffalo or Deer Dance; May 3, Feast of Santa Cruz Foot Race and Corn Dance; June 13, Feast of San Antonio Corn Dance; June 24, Feast of San Juan Corn Dance; second weekend in July, Taos Pueblo Powwow; July 25–26, Feast of Santa Ana and Santiago Corn Dance; September 29–30, Feast of San Geronimo Sunset Dance; December 24, Vespers and Bonfire Procession; December 25, Deer Dance or Matachines. While you're at the pueblo, respect the RESTRICTED AREA signs that protect the privacy of residents and native religious sites; do not enter private homes or open any

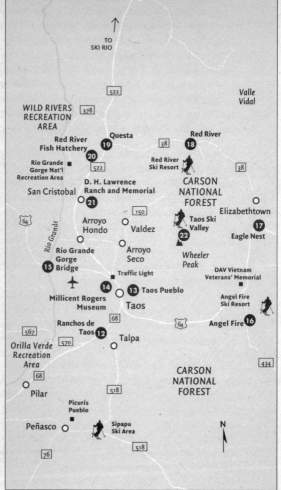

doors not clearly labeled as curio shops; do not photograph tribal members without asking permission; do not enter the cemetery grounds; and do not wade in the Rio Pueblo de Taos, which is considered sacred and is the community's sole source of drinking water. *Head to the right off Paseo del Pueblo Norte just past Best Western Kachina Lodge, tel. 505/758–1028, www. taospueblo.com. Tourist fees $10. Guided tours by appointment. Still-camera permit $10 (note: cameras that may look commercial, such as those with telephoto lenses, might be denied a permit); video-camera permit $20. Commercial photography, sketching, or painting only by prior permission from governor's office (505/758–1028); fees vary; apply at least 10 days in advance. Apr.–Nov., daily 8–4; Oct.–Mar., daily 8:30–4. Closed for funerals, religious ceremonies, and for a 2-month "quiet time" in late winter or early spring, and the last part of Aug.; call ahead before visiting at these times.*

NEED A
BREAK?
Look for signs that read FRY BREAD on dwellings in the pueblo: you can enter the kitchen and buy a piece of fresh bread dough that is flattened and deep-fried until puffy and golden brown and then topped with honey or powdered sugar.

THE ENCHANTED CIRCLE

The Enchanted Circle is an 84-mi loop north from Taos and back to town (U.S. 64 to NM 522 to NM 38 back to U.S. 64). The drive rings Wheeler Peak, New Mexico's highest mountain, and takes you through glorious panoramas of alpine valleys and the towering mountains of the lush Carson National Forest. You can see all the major sights in one day, or take a more leisurely tour and stay overnight.

Numbers in the text correspond to numbers in the margin and on the Taos Environs and the Enchanted Circle map.

What to See

16 ANGEL FIRE. Named for its blazing sunrise and sunset colors by the Ute Indians, who gathered here each autumn, Angel Fire is known these days primarily as a ski resort. In the summer there are arts and music events as well as hiking, river rafting, and ballooning. A prominent landmark is the **DAV Vietnam Veterans Memorial**, a 50-ft-high wing-shape monument built in 1971 by D. Victor Westphall, whose son David was killed in Vietnam. *U.S. 64, 25 mi east of Taos, tel. 505/377–6900 or 800/446–8117, angelfirenm.com.*

21 D. H. LAWRENCE RANCH AND MEMORIAL. The influential and controversial English writer David Herbert Lawrence and his wife, Frieda, arrived in Taos at the invitation of Mabel Dodge Luhan, who collected famous writers and artists the way some people collect butterflies. Luhan provided them a place to live, Kiowa Ranch, on 160 acres in the mountains. Rustic and remote, it's known as the D. H. Lawrence Ranch, though Lawrence never actually owned it. Lawrence lived in Taos on and off for about 22 months during a three-year period between 1922 and 1925. He wrote his novel *The Plumed Serpent* (1926), as well as some of his finest short stories and poetry, while in Taos and on excursions to Mexico. The houses here, owned by the University of New Mexico, are not open to the public, but you can go in the small cabin where Dorothy Brett, the Lawrences' traveling companion, stayed. You can also visit the D. H. Lawrence Memorial, a short walk up Lobo Mountain. A white shedlike structure, it's simple and unimposing. The writer fell ill while in France and died in a sanitorium there in 1930. Five years later Frieda had Lawrence's body disinterred and cremated and brought his ashes back to Taos. Frieda Lawrence is buried, as was her wish, in front of the memorial. *NM 522 (follow signed dirt road from the highway), San Cristobal, tel. 505/776–2245. Free. Daily dawn–dusk.*

17 EAGLE NEST. Thousands of acres of national forest surround this rustic village, population 189, elevation 8,090 ft. The shops and other buildings here evoke New Mexico's mining heritage, while a 1950s-style diner, Kaw-Lija's, serves up a memorable burger. *NM 38, 14 mi north of Angel Fire, tel. 505/377–2420 or 800/494–9117, www.eaglenestnm.com.*

⑲ QUESTA. Literally "hill," in the heart of the Sangre de Cristo Mountains, Questa is a quiet village about 12 mi from the town of Red River, nestled against the Red River itself and amid some of the most striking mountain country in New Mexico. **St. Anthony's Church,** built of adobe with 5-ft-thick walls and viga ceilings, is on the main street. Questa's **Cabresto Lake,** in Carson National Forest, is about 8 mi from town. Follow NM 563 to Forest Route 134, then 2 mi of a primitive road (134A)—you'll need a four-wheel-drive vehicle. You can trout fish and boat here from about June to October.

⑱ RED RIVER. A major ski resort, elevation 8,750 ft, Red River came into being as a miners' boomtown during the 19th century, taking its name from the river whose mineral content gives it a rosy color. When the gold petered out, Red River died, only to be rediscovered in the 1920s by migrants escaping the dust storms in the Great Plains. An Old West flavor remains: Main Street shoot-outs, an authentic melodrama, and square dancing and two-stepping are among the diversions here. Because of its many country dances and festivals, Red River is affectionately called "the New Mexico Home of the Texas Two-Step." The bustling little downtown area contains shops and sportswear boutiques. There is good fishing to be had in the Red River itself, and excellent alpine and Nordic skiing in the surrounding forest. *Off NM 38, tel. 505/774–2366 or 800/348–6444, www.redrivernm.com.*

NEED A BREAK? In Red River stop by the **SUNDANCE** (High St., tel. 505/754–2971) for Mexican food. **TEXAS RED'S STEAKHOUSE** (Main St., tel. 505/754–2922) has steaks, chops, burgers, and chicken.

✋ ⑳ **RED RIVER HATCHERY.** Freshwater trout are raised here to stock waters in Questa, Red River, Taos, Raton, and Las Vegas. You can feed them and learn how they're hatched, reared, stocked, and controlled. The visitor center has displays and exhibits, a fishing pond, and a machine that dispenses fish food. The self-guided tour can last anywhere from 20 to 90 minutes, depending on how enraptured you become. There's a picnic area and camping on the grounds. NM 522, 5 mi south of Questa, tel. 505/586-0222. Free. Daily 8-5.

TAOS SKI VALLEY

㉒ C.R. 150, 22 mi northeast of Taos.

A trip to Taos Ski Valley begins at the traffic light where you turn right onto NM 150 (Taos Ski Valley Road) from U.S. 64. Along the way, the hamlet of Arroyo Seco, some 5 mi up NM 150 from the traffic light, is worth a stop for lunch or ice cream and a look at crafts and antiques shops. Beyond Arroyo Seco the road crosses a high plain, then plunges into the Rio Hondo Canyon to follow the cascading brook upstream through the forest to Taos Ski Valley, where NM 150 ends. (It does not continue to Red River, as some disappointed motorists discover.)

Skiers from around the world return to the slopes and hospitality of the Village of Taos Ski Valley every year. This world-class area is known for its alpine village atmosphere, perhaps the finest ski school in the country, and the variety of its 72 runs. The valley also attracts outdoor enthusiasts with good hiking in summer and fall. Some of the best trails in Carson National Forest begin at the Village of Taos Ski Valley and go though dense woodland up to alpine tundra. There aren't many summer visitors, so you can have the trails up to Bull-of-the-Woods, Gold Hill, Williams Lake, Italianos, and Wheeler Peak nearly all to yourself. Easy nature hikes are organized by the Bavarian hotel, guided by Shar Sharghi, a botanist and horticulturist. Special events like barn dances and wine tastings occur throughout the nonskiing seasons.

EATING OUT

For a place as remote as Taos, the dining scene is surprisingly varied. You can find the usual coffee shops and Mexican-style eateries but also restaurants serving creatively prepared Continental, Italian, and southwestern cuisine.

DOWNTOWN TAOS

American

$$ OGELVIE'S BAR AND GRILL. On the second floor of an old two-story adobe building, Ogelvie's is the perfect spot for people-watching from on high, especially from the outdoor patio in summer. You won't find any culinary surprises here, just dependable meat-and-potato dishes. The sure bets are Angus beef, lamb sirloin, and meat or cheese enchiladas. *East side of Taos Plaza, tel. 505/758–8866. Reservations not accepted. AE, DC, MC, V.*

American/Casual

$ MICHAEL'S KITCHEN. This casual, homey restaurant serves up a bit of everything—you can order a hamburger while your friend who can't get enough chile can order another enchilada. Brunch is popular with the locals, and amusing asides to the waitstaff over the intercom contribute to the energetic buzz. Breakfast, lunch, and dinner are served daily, but be sure to order dinner by 8:30 PM. *304 Paseo del Pueblo Norte, tel. 505/758–4178. Reservations not accepted. AE, D, MC, V.*

taos dining

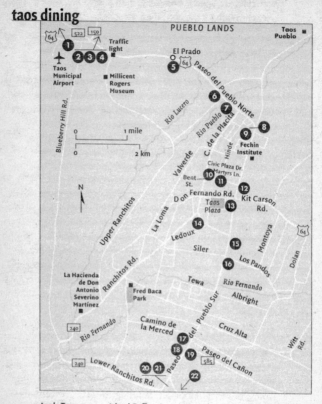

Cafés

$ DRAGONFLY CAFÉ. This breakfast and lunch café bakes its own bread and serves large and tasty omelets, Swedish pancakes, Vietnamese chicken salad, and panini sandwiches. You can sit out front when it's warm and watch the tourists go by. 402 *Paseo del Pueblo Norte, tel. 505/737–5859. MC, V.*

Contemporary

$$$–$$$$ APPLE TREE. Named for the large tree in the umbrella-shaded courtyard, this is a great lunch and dinner spot in a historic adobe a block from the Plaza. Among the well-crafted dishes are barbecued duck fajitas and mango chicken enchiladas. The restaurant has received regular awards for its wine selection, which includes many options by the glass. Sunday brunch is served from 11 to 3. Expect about a 15-minute wait if you don't have a reservation. 123 *Bent St., tel. 505/758–1900. AE, D, DC, MC, V.*

$$–$$$$ DOC MARTIN'S. The restaurant of the Taos Inn takes its name from the building's original owner, a local physician who performed operations and delivered babies in rooms that are now the dining areas. Try the piñon-crusted salmon and the Aztec chocolate mousse with roasted-banana sauce. The wine list has won awards from *Wine Spectator* and other organizations. Taos Inn, 125 *Paseo del Pueblo Norte, tel. 505/758–1977. MC, V.*

$$–$$$$ LAMBERT'S OF TAOS. The signature dishes at this restaurant 2½ blocks south of the Plaza include curried crab cakes and pepper-crusted lamb. California's finest vintages receive top billing on the wine list. 309 *Paseo del Pueblo Sur, tel. 505/758–1009. AE, DC, MC, V. No lunch.*

$$$ BYZANTIUM. Off a grassy courtyard near the Blumenschein and Harwood museums, this restaurant offers an eclectic menu with touches of Asia, the Middle East, and Europe in dishes such as

Asian seafood cakes, duck curry, and vegetable potpie. *Ledoux St. and La Placita, tel.* 505/751–0805. *AE, MC, V. Closed Tues.–Wed. No lunch.*

$$–$$$ **LA LUNA.** In a colorful two-level space with a mural along one wall, the former New Yorkers who own the place have attracted a local clientele fond of the pasta dishes (like penne with cilantro-citrus sauce), the daily fish specials, and pizza from the wood-fired oven. Also for sale: the house apple-balsamic vinaigrette and salsa. *225 Paseo del Pueblo Sur, tel.* 505/751–0023. *AE, D, MC, V. No lunch Sun.*

$–$$ **BRAVO!** This restaurant and full bar inside an upscale grocery store and beer and wine shop is a great stop for gourmet picnic fixings or an on-site meal. You can feast on anything from a turkey sandwich to Louisiana crawfish—and there's a children's menu to boot. The beer and wine selection is formidable. *1353A Paseo del Pueblo Sur, tel.* 505/758–8100. *Reservations not accepted. MC, V. Closed Sun.*

Deli

$$ **BENT STREET DELI.** Great soups, sandwiches, salads, and desserts are the trademarks of the unassuming Bent Street Deli, which serves beer, wine, and gourmet coffees. Reubens are on the menu for East Coasters and others who can't live without a dose of pastrami. Dinners are a little fancier: fresh salmon, pork loin with red wine mushroom glaze, and shrimp in pesto sauce. Breakfast is served until 11 AM. *120 Bent St., tel.* 505/758–5787. *MC, V. Closed Sun.*

Hawaiian

$–$$ **ISLAND COFFEES & HAWAIIAN GRILL.** If you're tired of burritos, stop in at Island Coffees for Maui crab cakes or mango coconut chicken. Lots of noodle dishes and stir fries are on the menu, along with Kona coffees. You can even check your e-mail or surf the Web. Breakfast is available from 6:30 AM. *1032 Paseo del Pueblo Sur, tel.* 505/758–7777. *MC, V. Closed Sun.*

Middle Eastern

$ SHEVA CAFÉ. Delectable falafel, eggplant salad, and stuffed grape leaves served with homemade pita bread have made this vegetarian café a local favorite. The friendly Israeli staff will make you feel at home. 812B *Paseo del Pueblo Norte, tel. 505/737–9290. No credit cards. No dinner Fri.–Sat.*

Southwestern

$ GUADALAJARA GRILL. Tasty Mexican cuisine is the feature here, served quickly from the open, spotless kitchens and popular enough with local patrons that there is one on each end of town. You'll hear Spanish banter across the kitchen counter while you watch your burritos or enchiladas being prepared. 822 *Paseo del Pueblo Norte, tel. 505/737–0816; 1384 Paseo del Pueblo Sur, tel. 505/ 751–0063. MC, V.*

$ ORLANDO'S. This family-run local favorite features authentic-tasting *carne adovada* (red chile–marinated pork), blue-corn enchiladas, and an innovative shrimp burrito, among other offerings. Eat in the cozy dining room or call ahead for takeout. 114 *Don Juan Valdez La., off Paseo del Pueblo Norte, tel. 505/751–1450. No credit cards. Closed Sun.*

SOUTH OF TAOS

American

$$$–$$$$ STAKEOUT GRILL AND BAR. On Outlaw Hill in the foothills of the Sangre de Cristo Mountains, this old adobe homestead has 100-mi-long views and sunsets that dazzle. The sturdy fare includes New York strip steaks, Alaskan crab legs, swordfish steaks, duck, chicken, and daily pasta specials. The restaurant's decor will take you back to the days of the Wild West, even though the owners hail from northern Italy. *Stakeout Dr., 8½ mi south of Taos Plaza, east of NM 68 (look for cowboy sign), tel. 505/751–3815. AE, D, DC, MC, V.*

Contemporary

$$$–$$$$ **JOSEPH'S TABLE.** Widely acclaimed Joseph's is a rustic, dramatic
★ stage for carefully prepared fare like grilled corn chipotle aioli with
cotija cheese, duck breast on corn pudding, and pepper steak with
garlic-mashed red potatoes. The first-rate desserts are more
ornate. *4167 Paseo del Pueblo Sur (NM 68), Ranchos de Taos, tel. 505/
751–4512. AE, D, DC, MC, V.*

$$$–$$$$ **TRADING POST CAFE.** A western ambience, impeccable service,
★ and an imaginative menu have made the Trading Post a popular
dining spot in Ranchos. The marinated salmon gravlax appetizer
is exceptional, and the paella is a bounty for two. Try the homemade
raspberry sorbet or the flan. To park, turn east onto Hwy. 518 (Talpa
Road) just north of the restaurant, and then walk back along
Talpa Road to get to the entrance. *4179 Paseo del Pueblo Sur (NM
68), Ranchos de Taos, tel. 505/758–5089. D, DC, MC, V. Closed Sun.*

NORTH OF TAOS

Cafés

$ **TAOS COW.** Not only is it headquarters for ice cream made from
growth-hormone-free cows (featured in area health food stores),
but this place will serve you coffee, chai, breakfast, and lunch.
Favorites among the three dozen ice cream flavors are cherry
ristra, piñon caramel, and the true test—vanilla. *591 Hondo Seco
Rd., Arroyo Seco, tel. 505/776–5640. MC, V.*

Contemporary

$$$$ **MOMENTITOS DE LA VIDA.** Chef Chris Maher's restaurant brings
★ an ambitious, worldly focus to dining out in the area. Outstanding
food and wine are served in elegant surroundings. An evening's
entrée might be apricot-glazed Cornish hen or pistachio-encrusted
rack of lamb, but save room for desserts, which change nightly.
There's live music in the piano bar several nights a week. Sunday

brunch allows those on a tighter budget to enjoy the food and atmosphere. *Taos Ski Valley Rd. (S.R. 150), tel. 505/776–3333. AE, MC, V. Closed Mon. No lunch.*

Italian

$$$ **VILLA FONTANA.** Entering this restaurant, which serves northern
★ Italian cuisine, is like walking into a sophisticated Italian country inn: warm coral walls, candlelight, gleaming hardwood tables, starched linens, and courtly service. Notable dishes include cream of wild mushroom soup, osso buco, and fresh fish and game. Lunch is served in the garden. *NM 522, 5 mi north of Taos Plaza, Arroyo Hondo, tel. 505/758–5800. AE, D, DC, MC, V. Closed Sun. No lunch Nov.–May.*

Southwestern

$$–$$$ **OLD BLINKING LIGHT.** Just past the landmark "old blinking light" (now a regular stoplight), this rambling adobe is known for its steaks, ribs, and margaritas. In summer you can sit out in the walled garden and take in the spectacular mountain view. There's a wine shop on the premises. *Ski Valley Rd., El Prado, tel. 505/776–8787. AE, MC, V.*

SHOPPING

Retail options in Taos Plaza consist mostly of T-shirt emporiums and souvenir shops that are easily bypassed, though a few stores, like Blue Rain Gallery, carry quality Native American artifacts and jewelry. The more upscale galleries and boutiques are two short blocks north on Bent Street, including the John Dunn House Shops. Kit Carson Road, also known as U.S. 64, has a mix of the old and the new. There's metered municipal parking downtown, though the traffic can be daunting. Some shops worth checking out are in St. Francis Plaza in Ranchos de Taos, 4 mi south of the Plaza near the San Francisco de Asís Church.

ART GALLERIES

For at least a century, artists have been drawn to Taos by its special light, open space, and natural grandeur. The result is a vigorous art community with some 80 galleries, a lively market, and an estimated 1,000 residents producing art full- or part-time. Many artists explore themes of the western landscape, Native Americans, and adobe architecture; others create abstract forms and mixed-media works that may or may not reflect the Southwest. Some local artists grew up in Taos, but many—Anglo, Hispanic, and Native Americans—are adopted Taoseños.

BLUE RAIN GALLERY (117 S. Plaza, tel. 505/751–0066) carries some of the finest examples of Pueblo pottery and Hopi katsina dolls to be found anywhere, ranging in price from several hundred to several thousand dollars. The owner, Leroy Garcia, takes time to explain the materials and traditions. The gallery also sells Indian-made jewelry and art.

CLAY AND FIBER GALLERY (201 Paseo del Pueblo Sur, tel. 505/758–8093) has exhibited first-rate ceramics, glass, pottery, and hand-painted silks and weavings by local artists for the past quarter century.

FENIX GALLERY (228B Paseo del Pueblo Norte, tel. 505/758–9120) is a showcase for contemporary art, exhibiting paintings, sculpture, ceramics, and lithography by established Taos artists.

GALLERY ELENA (111 Morada La., tel. 505/758–9094) shows the works of Veloy, Dan, and Michael Vigil.

INGER JIRBY GALLERY (207 Ledoux St., tel. 505/758–7333) displays the landscapes and interiors of colorist Jirby.

LAS COMADRES (228A Paseo del Pueblo Sur, tel. 505/737–5323) is a women's cooperative gallery showing arts and crafts.

LEO WEAVER JEWELRY GALLERIES represents 50 local jewelry artists at two locations (62 St. Francis Plaza, Ranchos de Taos, tel. 505/751–1003; Historic Taos Inn, 125 Paseo del Pueblo Norte, tel. 505/758–8171). You'll find contemporary and traditional designs in silver, gold, and precious stones, as well as beautiful silver disk concha belts.

LUMINA GALLERY (239 Morada La., tel. 505/758–7282) exhibits paintings by artists who have worked in New Mexico for at least 20 years, as well as sculpture, photography, and antiques. Artists represented include Joe Waldrun and Chuck Henningsen. The gallery is in the former adobe home of Victor Higgins, one of the original members of the Taos Society of Artists. The outdoor sculpture garden is a serene oasis.

MICHAEL MCCORMICK GALLERY (106C Paseo del Pueblo Norte, tel. 505/758–1372) is home to the sensual, stylized female portraits by Miguel Martinez and the architectural paintings of Margaret Nes. The adjacent JD Challenger studio and gallery displays the artist's paintings of Native Americans.

MISSION GALLERY (138 E. Kit Carson Rd., tel. 505/758–2861) carries the works of early Taos artists, early New Mexico Modernists, and important contemporary artists. The gallery is in the former home of painter Joseph H. Sharp.

NAVAJO GALLERY (210 Ledoux St., tel. 505/758–3250) shows the works of owner and Navajo painter and sculptor R. C. Gorman, well known for his ethereal interpretations of Indian imagery.

NEW DIRECTIONS GALLERY (107B N. Plaza, tel. 505/758–2771 or 800/658–6903) displays works by contemporary Taos artists such as Larry Bell, Ted Egri, and Maya Torres in a light-filled room.

PARKS GALLERY (140 Kit Carson Rd., tel. 505/751–0343) specializes in contemporary paintings, sculptures, and prints. Mixed-media artist Melissa Zink shows here, as well as painter Jim Wagner.

R. B. RAVENS GALLERY (St. Francis Plaza, Ranchos de Taos, tel. 505/758–7322) exhibits paintings by the founding artists of Taos, pre-1930s weavings, and ceramics.

SIX DIRECTIONS (129B N. Plaza, tel. 505/758–5844) has paintings, alabaster and bronze sculpture, Native American artifacts, silver jewelry, and pottery. Bill Rabbit and Robert Redbird are among the artists represented here.

SPECIALTY STORES

Books

BRODSKY BOOKSHOP (226B Paseo del Pueblo Norte, tel. 505/758–9468) has new and used books—contemporary literature, southwestern classics, children's titles—piled every which way, but the amiable proprietor will help you find what you need.

FERNANDEZ DE TAOS BOOK STORE (109 N. Plaza, tel. 505/758–4391) carries magazines, major out-of-town newspapers, and many books on southwestern culture and history.

G. ROBINSON OLD PRINTS AND MAPS (John Dunn House, 124D Bent St., tel. 505/758–2278) stocks rare books, Edward Curtis photographs, and maps and prints from the 16th to 19th century.

MERLIN'S GARDEN (127 Bent St., tel. 505/758–0985) is a funky repository of metaphysical books and literature from Ram Dass to Thomas More. The shop also carries tapes, incense, crystals, and jewelry.

MOBY DICKENS (John Dunn House, 124A Bent St., tel. 505/758–3050), great for browsing, is a bookstore for all ages. It carries many books on the Southwest as well as a large stock of general-interest books.

MYSTERY INK (121 Camino de la Placita, tel. 505/751–1092) specializes in high-quality used books, especially murder mysteries. The shop also carries some foreign-language literature.

TAOS BOOK SHOP (122D Kit Carson Rd., tel. 505/758–3733), the oldest bookshop in New Mexico, founded in 1947, specializes in out-of-print and southwestern books. The founders, Genevieve Janssen and Claire Morrill, compiled the reminiscences of their Taos years in *A Taos Mosaic* (University of New Mexico Press).

Clothing

LA LANA WOOLS (136 Paseo del Pueblo Norte, tel. 505/758–9631) carries exquisite handwoven and hand-knit wearables, as well as plant-dyed yarns.

OVERLAND SHEEPSKIN COMPANY (NM 522, 100-A McCarthy Plaza, tel. 505/758–8822, tel. 505/758–5150) carries high-quality sheepskin coats, hats, mittens, and slippers, many with Taos beadwork.

TAOS MOCCASIN CO. FACTORY OUTLET (216B Paseo del Pueblo Sur, tel. 800/747–7025) sells moccasins made in the building next door—everything from booties for babies to men's high and low boots—at great discounts.

Collectibles

HORSE FEATHERS (109B Kit Carson Rd.,, tel. 505/758–7457) is a fun collection of cowboy antiques and vintage western wear—boots, hats, buckles, jewelry, and all manner of paraphernalia.

Home Furnishings

ABYDOS (7036 S.R. 518, Talpa, tel. 505/758–0483) sells fine handmade New Mexican–style furniture.

ALHAMBRA (124 Paseo del Pueblo Sur, tel. 505/758–4161) carries a lovely collection of antiques, Oriental rugs and textiles, and South Asian artifacts.

CAMINO REAL IMPORTS (1305A Paseo del Pueblo Norte, tel. 505/758–7999), 2½ mi north of the Taos Plaza, has rooms full of Mexican artifacts, like serapes, clay pots, tin ornaments, knitwear, ponchos, blankets, and handpainted tiles and sinks.

CASA CRISTAL POTTERY (1306 Paseo del Pueblo Norte, tel. 505/758–1530), 2½ mi north of the Taos Plaza, has a huge stock of stoneware, serapes, clay pots, Native American ironwood carvings, fountains, sweaters, ponchos, clay fireplaces, Mexican blankets, tiles, piñatas, and blue glassware from Guadalajara.

CASA DEL SOL (1638 Paseo del Pueblo Norte, tel. 505/758–7496), north of town near the intersection of NM 150, is a warehouse of Mexican imports like straw and tin ornaments, clay pots, shawls, ponchos, clay fireplaces, blankets, tiles, and piñatas.

COUNTRY FURNISHINGS OF TAOS (534 Paseo del Pueblo Norte, tel. 505/758–4633) sells folk art from northern New Mexico, handmade furniture, metalwork lamps and beds, and colorful accessories.

FLYING CARPET (208 Ranchitos Rd., tel. 505/751–4035) carries colorful rugs and kilims from Turkey, Kurdistan, Persia, and elsewhere. Owner Bill Eagleton, who wrote a book about Kurdish carpets, and his wife, Kay, have a keen eye for quality and design.

FRANZETTI METALWORKS (120G Bent St., tel. 505/758–7872) displays owner Pozzi Franzetti's whimsical steelwork designs— from switch plate covers to wall hangings in animal and western motifs.

JOHN BOSSHARD TRIBAL AND TRADITIONAL ARTS (112C Camino de la Placita, tel. 505/751–9445) stocks antiques and artworks from the Southwest and around the world.

LA UNICA COSA (117 Paseo del Pueblo Norte, tel. 505/758–3065) has a striking collection of Zapotec Indian rugs and hangings.

LOS ANCESTROS (66 St. Francis Plaza, Ranchos de Taos, tel. 505/737–5053) stocks Spanish-colonial reproductions and accessories.

TAOS BLUE (101A Bent St., tel. 505/758–3561) carries jewelry, pottery, and contemporary works by Native Americans (masks, rattles, sculpture), as well as Hispanic *santos* (*bultos* and *retablos*).

The **TAOS COMPANY** (124K Bent St., tel. 800/548–1141) sells magnificent Spanish-style furniture, chandeliers, rugs, and textiles; Mexican *equipal* (wood and leather) chairs; and other accessories.

TAOS TINWORKS (1204D Paseo del Pueblo Norte, tel. 505/758–9724) sells handcrafted tinwork such as wall sconces, mirrors, lamps, and table ornaments by Marion Moore.

WEAVING SOUTHWEST (216B Paseo del Pueblo Norte, tel. 505/758–0433) represents 25 tapestry artists who make beautiful rugs, blankets, and pillows. The store also sells supplies for weavers.

Native American Arts and Crafts

ALL ONE TRIBE (Taos, tel. 800/442–3786) is a co-op of Native American master drum makers who sell hand-painted, signed instruments.

BUFFALO DANCER (103A E. Plaza, tel. 505/758–8718) buys, sells, and trades Native American arts and crafts, including pottery, belts, katsina dolls, hides, and silver-coin jewelry.

DON FERNANDO CURIOS AND GIFTS (104 W. Plaza, tel. 505/758–3791), which opened in 1938 (it's the oldest Native American arts shop on the Taos Plaza), sells good turquoise jewelry, katsinas, straw baskets, and colorful beads.

EL RINCÓN (114 E. Kit Carson Rd., tel. 505/758–9188) is housed in a large, dark, cluttered century-old adobe. Native American items of all kinds are bought and sold here: drums, feathered headdresses, Navajo rugs, beads, bowls, baskets, shields, beaded moccasins, jewelry, arrows, and spearheads. The packed back room contains Indian, Hispanic, and Anglo Wild West artifacts.

SOUTHWEST MOCCASIN & DRUM (803 Paseo del Pueblo Norte, tel. 505/758–9332 or 800/447–3630) has a large selection of native moccasins and drums, many painted by local artists.

TAOS DRUMS (Santa Fe Hwy./NM 68, tel. 505/758–9844 or 800/424–3786) is the factory outlet for the Taos Drum Factory. The store, 5 mi south of Taos Plaza (look for the large tepee), stocks handmade Pueblo log drums, leather lamp shades, and wrought-iron and southwestern furniture.

TAOS GENERAL STORE (223C Paseo del Pueblo Sur, tel. 505/758–9051) stocks a large selection of furniture and decorative items from around the world, as well as American Indian pots, rugs, and jewelry.

Sporting Goods

ANDEAN SOFTWEAR (118 Sutton Pl., Taos Ski Valley, tel. 505/776–2508) carries exotic clothing, textiles, and jewelry. Note the deliciously soft alpaca sweaters from Peru.

COTTAM'S SKI AND OUTDOOR (207A Paseo del Pueblo Sur, tel. 505/758–2822) carries hiking and backpacking gear, maps, fishing licenses and supplies, and ski equipment.

LOS RIOS ANGLERS (226C Paseo del Pueblo Norte, tel. 505/758–2798 or 800/748–1707) is a fly-fisherman's haven for fly rods, flies, clothing, books, instruction, and guide service to local streams.

MUDD 'N' FLOOD MOUNTAIN SHOP (134 Bent St., tel. 505/751–9100) has gear and clothing for rock climbers, backpackers, campers, and backcountry skiers.

TAOS MOUNTAIN OUTFITTERS (114 S. Plaza, tel. 505/758–9292) has supplies for kayakers, skiers, climbers, and backpackers, as well as maps, books, and handy advice.

OUTDOOR ACTIVITIES AND SPORTS

Whether you plan to cycle around town, jog along Paseo del Pueblo Norte, or play a few rounds of golf, keep in mind that the altitude in Taos is over 7,000 ft. It's best to keep physical exertion to a minimum until your body becomes acclimated to the altitude—a full day to a few days, depending on your constitution. With the decreased oxygen and humidity, you may experience some or all of the following symptoms: headache, nausea, insomnia, shortness of breath, diarrhea, sleeplessness, and tension. If you are planning to engage in physical activity, avoid alcohol and coffee (which aggravate "high-altitude syndrome") and drink a lot of water and juice. Some locals also recommend taking aspirin in the morning and afternoon.

CARSON NATIONAL FOREST surrounds Taos and spans almost 200 mi across northern New Mexico encompassing mountains, lakes, streams, villages, and much of the Enchanted Circle. Hiking, cross-country skiing, horseback riding, mountain biking, backpacking, trout fishing, boating, and wildflower viewing are among the popular activities here. The forest is home to big-game animals and many species of smaller animals and songbirds. You can drive into the forest land via Hwys. 522, 150, 38, and 578. Contact the Carson National Forest for maps, safety guidelines, and conditions (it's open weekdays 8–4:30). *Forest Service Building, 208 Cruz Alta Rd., Taos 87571, tel. 505/758–6200.*

PARTICIPANT SPORTS

Ballooning

PARADISE BALLOONS (tel. 505/751–6098) and **PUEBLO BALLOONS** (tel. 505/751–9877) conduct balloon rides over and into the Rio Grande gorge at sunrise or by moonlight. The cost is $195 plus gratuities.

Bicycling

Taos-area roads are steep and hilly, and none have marked bicycle lanes, so be careful while cycling. The West Rim Trail offers a fairly flat but view-studded 9-mi ride that follows the Rio Grande canyon's west rim from the Rio Grande Gorge Bridge to near the Taos Junction Bridge.

"GEARING UP" BICYCLE SHOP (129 Paseo del Pueblo Sur, tel. 505/751–0365) is a full-service bike shop that also has information about tours and guides. **NATIVE SONS ADVENTURES** (1033A Paseo del Pueblo Sur, tel. 505/758–3392 or 800/753–7559) offers guided tours on its mountain bikes.

Fishing

Carson National Forest has some of the best trout fishing in New Mexico. Its streams and lakes are home to rainbow, brown, and native Rio Grande cutthroat trout.

In Taos, **LOS RIOS ANGLERS** (226C Paseo del Pueblo Norte, tel. 505/758–2798 or 800/748–1707) offers free one-hour fly-casting clinics, weekly between May and August. **SOLITARY ANGLER** (204B Paseo del Pueblo Norte, tel. 505/758–5653 or 866/502–1700) guides fly-fishing expeditions that search out uncrowded habitats. Well-known area fishing guide **TAYLOR STREIT** (tel. 505/751–1312) takes individuals or small groups out for fishing and lessons.

Golf

The 18-hole, par-72 course at the **ANGEL FIRE COUNTRY CLUB** (Country Club Dr. off NM 434, Angel Fire, tel. 505/377–3055), one of the highest in the nation, is open from May to mid-October. The greens fee is $35; an optional cart costs $12.50 per person. The greens fee at the 18-hole, PGA-rated, par-72 championship course at **TAOS COUNTRY CLUB** (Hwy. 570, Ranchos de Taos, tel. 505/758–7300 or 888/826–7465) ranges from $25 to $42; optional carts cost $22.

Health Clubs and Fitness Centers

The **NORTHSIDE HEALTH & FITNESS CENTER** (1307 Paseo del Pueblo Norte, tel. 505/751–1242) is a spotlessly clean facility with indoor and outdoor pools, a hot tub, tennis courts, and aerobics classes. Nonmembers pay $9 per day; passes for a week or longer are also available. The center provides paid child care with a certified Montessori teacher. About 3 mi south of the Plaza, **TAOS SPA & TENNIS CLUB** (111 Doña Ana Dr., tel. 888/758–1981) has tennis and racquetball courts, indoor and outdoor pools, fitness equipment, saunas, steam rooms, and hot tubs, as well as baby-sitting and massage services. Nonmembers pay $10 per day. The **TAOS YOUTH AND FAMILY CENTER** (1005 Camino de Colores, tel. 505/758–4160) has an outdoor Olympic-size ice arena, where rollerblading, volleyball, and basketball take place in summer. Other scheduled activities are open to the public.

Hiking

Carson National Forest has hundreds of miles of trails that wind through diverse terrain. Strenuous trails lead to Wheeler Peak, the highest point in New Mexico, at 13,161 ft. Gentler paths head up other piney and meadow-filled mountains like Gold Hill or past old mining camps. For canyon climbing, head into the rocky Rio Grande gorge. The best entry point into the gorge is at the Wild River Recreation Area in Cerro, 35 mi north of Taos.

If you're coming from a lower altitude, you should take time to acclimatize, and all hikers should follow basic safety procedures. Wind, cold, and wetness can occur any time of year, and the mountain climate produces sudden storms. Dress in layers and wear sturdy footwear; carry water, food, sunscreen, hat, sunglasses, and a first-aid kit. Contact the Forest Service for maps of hiking trails. The **BUREAU OF LAND MANAGEMENT, TAOS RESOURCE AREA OFFICE** (226 Cruz Alta, Taos, tel. 505/758–8851) can help with hiking information.

River Rafting

The Taos Box, at the bottom of the steep-walled canyon far below the Rio Grande Gorge Bridge, is the granddaddy of thrilling white water in New Mexico and is best attempted by experts only—or on a guided trip—but the river also offers more placid sections such as through the Orilla Verde Recreation Area. Spring runoff is the busy season, from mid-April through June, but rafting companies conduct tours March to November. Shorter two-hour options usually cover the fairly tame section of the river. The **BUREAU OF LAND MANAGEMENT, TAOS RESOURCE AREA OFFICE** (226 Cruz Alta, tel. 505/758–8851) has a list of registered river guides and information about running the river on your own.

BIG RIVER RAFT TRIPS (tel. 505/758–9711 or 800/748–3760) offers dinner float trips and rapids runs. **FAR FLUNG ADVENTURES** (tel. 505/758–2628 or 800/359–2627) operates half-day, full-day, and overnight rafting trips along the Rio Grande and the Rio Chama. **LOS RIOS RIVER RUNNERS** (tel. 505/776–8854 or 800/544–1181) will take you to your choice of spots—the Rio Chama, the Lower Gorge, or the Taos Box. **NATIVE SONS ADVENTURES** (715 Paseo del Pueblo Sur, tel. 505/758–9342 or 800/753–7559) offers several trip options on the Rio Grande. **RIO GRANDE RIVER TOURS** (tel. 505/758–0762 or 800/525–4966) runs trips through Pilar Canyon and the Lower Rio Grande gorge.

Skiing

The six ski areas within 90 mi of Taos have beginning, intermediate, and advanced slopes and snowmobile and cross-country skiing trails. All the resorts have fine accommodations and safe child-care programs at reasonable prices. Only Taos Ski Valley prohibits snowboarding.

ANGEL FIRE RESORT is a busy ski destination, with 68 runs for all levels of skiers, 5 lifts, and a snowboarding slope. *N. Angel Fire Rd. off NM 434, Angel Fire, tel. 505/377–6401; 800/633–7463 outside New Mexico; www.angelfireresort.com. $43 a day. Mid-Dec.–early Apr.*

At the **ENCHANTED FOREST CROSS-COUNTRY SKI AREA,** 24 mi of groomed trails loop from the warming hut through meadows and pines in Carson Nation Forest, 3 mi east of Red River. *417 W. Main St. (Red River 87558), tel. 505/754–2374 or 800/966–9381, www.enchantedforestxc.com. $10 a day. Late Nov.–Easter.*

The **RED RIVER SKI AREA** is in the middle of the historic gold-mining town of Red River, with lifts within walking distance of restaurants and hotels. Slopes for all levels of skiers make the area popular with families, and there's a snowboarding park. *Pioneer Rd. off NM 38, Red River, tel. 505/754–2323, www. redriverskiarea.com. $43 a day. Late Nov.–Easter.*

SIPAPU LODGE AND SKI AREA (NM 518, Vadito, tel. 505/587–2240 or 800/587–2240, www.sipapunm.com) is open from mid-December to the end of March.

SKI RIO (NM 196 off NM 522, Costillo, tel. 505/758–7707), north of Taos Ski Valley, opens for daily business from mid-December to early April. The resort has 83 runs and makes its own snow.

With 72 runs and an average of 323 inches of annual snowfall, **TAOS SKI VALLEY** is justly popular. The slopes offer something for every level of skier: 51% (e.g. the ridge chutes, Al's Run,

Inferno) are for experts, 25% (e.g. Honeysuckle) are for intermediate skiers, and 24% (e.g. Bambi, Porcupine) are for beginners. There's no snowboarding. *Village of Taos Ski Valley, tel. 505/776–2291, www.skitaos.org. $49. Late Nov.–early Apr.*

Swimming

The **DON FERNANDO MUNICIPAL SWIMMING POOL** (120 Civic Plaza Dr., tel. 505/737–2622) is open weekdays 1–4:30 and weekends 1–5. Admission is $2.

SPECTATOR SPORTS

Sporting events in the Taos area include the Rodeo de Taos, which takes place at the Taos County Rodeo Fairgrounds in mid-June, and the Taos Mountain Balloon Rally, held in a field south of downtown during the last week in October. Contact the Taos County Chamber of Commerce (☞ Visitor Information in Practical Information, *below*) for more information.

NIGHTLIFE AND THE ARTS

Evening entertainment is modest in Taos. Some motels and hotels present solo musicians or small combos in their bars and lounges. Everything from down-home blues bands to Texas two-step dancing blossoms on Saturday and Sunday nights in winter. In summer things heat up during the week as well. For information about what's going on around town pick up *Taos Magazine*. The weekly *Taos News*, published on Thursday, carries arts and entertainment information in the "Tempo" section. The arts scene is much more lively, with festivals every season for nearly every taste.

NIGHTLIFE

Bars and Lounges

The **ADOBE BAR** (Taos Inn, 125 Paseo del Pueblo Norte, tel. 505/758–2233), a local meet-and-greet spot known as "Taos's living room," books talented acts, from solo guitarists to small folk groups and, two or three nights a week, jazz musicians. **FERNANDO'S HIDEAWAY** (Holiday Inn, 1005 Paseo del Pueblo Sur, tel. 505/758–4444) occasionally presents live entertainment—jazz, blues, hiphop, R&B, salsa, vocals, and country music. Saturday is reserved for karaoke. Lavish complimentary happy-hour buffets are laid out on weekday evenings.

Cabaret

The **KACHINA LODGE CABARET** (413 Paseo del Pueblo Norte, tel. 505/758–2275) brings in headline acts, such as Arlo Guthrie and the Dirty Dozen Brass Band, on a regular basis and has dancing.

Coffeehouse

CAFFE TAZZA (122 Kit Carson Rd., tel. 505/758–8706) presents free evening performances throughout the week—folk singing, jazz, blues, poetry, and fiction readings.

Country-and-Western

The **SAGEBRUSH INN** (1508 Paseo del Pueblo Sur, tel. 505/758–2254) hosts musicians and dancing in its lobby lounge. If you hear that South by Southwest is playing, check out the three-man band. There's no cover charge, and if you show up on a Thursday, you can learn to two-step.

Jazz and Dance Clubs

ALLEY CANTINA (121 Teresina La., tel. 505/758–2121) has jazz, folk, and blues—as well as shuffleboard and board games for those not moved to dance. The piano bar at **MOMENTITOS DE LA VIDA** (C.R. 150, Arroyo Seco, tel. 505/776–3333) often presents jazz and bossa nova. **THUNDERBIRD LODGE** (3 Thunderbird Rd., tel. 505/776–2280) in the Taos Ski Valley has free jazz nights and country-and-western swing dancing. **WESTERN SKY CAFÉ** (1398 Weimer Rd., tel. 505/751–7771) offers evenings of blues and jazz standards.

THE ARTS

Long a beacon for visual artists, Taos is also becoming a magnet for touring musicians, especially in the summer, when performers and audiences are drawn to the heady high desert atmosphere. Festivals celebrate the visual arts, music, poetry, and film.

The **TAOS ART ASSOCIATION** (133 Paseo del Pueblo Norte, tel. 505/758–2052) has information about art-related events in Taos. The **TAOS COMMUNITY AUDITORIUM** (145 Paseo del Pueblo Norte, tel. 505/758–4677) presents plays, dance, concerts, and movies.

The **TAOS SPRING ARTS FESTIVAL** (tel. 505/758–3873 or 800/732–8267, www.taosguide.com), held throughout Taos during the month of May, is a showcase for the visual, performing, and literary arts of the community and allows you to rub elbows with the many artists who call Taos home. The Mother's Day Arts and Crafts weekend during the festival always draws a crowd.

The **TAOS FALL ARTS FESTIVAL** (tel. 505/758–3873 or 800/732–8267, www.taosguide.com), from late September to early October, is the major arts gathering, when buyers are in town and many other events, such as a Taos Pueblo feast, take place.

The **TAOS POETRY CIRCUS** (www.poetrycircus.org) comes to town for a week every June, presenting a performance series that includes readings, seminars, slams, and the World Heavyweight Championship Poetry Bout. It includes events at Taos Pueblo with young Native American poets.

Film

TAOS TALKING PICTURE FESTIVAL (tel. 505/751–0637 or 800/267–0104, www.ttpix.org) is a multicultural celebration of cinema artists, with a focus on Native American film and video makers. The mid-April festival presents independent films, documentaries, animation, and some classic cinema.

Music

From mid-June to early August the Taos School of Music and the International Institute of Music fill the evenings with the sounds of chamber and symphonic orchestras at the **TAOS CHAMBER MUSIC FESTIVAL** (tel. 505/776–2388). Nearly four decades old, this is America's oldest chamber music summer program and possibly the largest assembly of professional musicians in the Southwest. Concerts are presented every Saturday evening, and every other Friday evening from mid-June to August, at the Taos Community Auditorium. Tickets cost $15. The events at Taos Ski Valley are free.

The Taos School of Music gives free weekly summer concerts and recitals from mid-June to early August at the **HOTEL SAINT BERNARD** (tel. 505/776–2251), at the mountain base (near the lifts) of Taos Ski Valley.

MUSIC FROM ANGEL FIRE (tel. 505/758–4667 or 505/377–3233) is a series of classical and jazz concerts presented at the Taos Community Auditorium and the Angel Fire Community Auditorium in the town center from late August to early September. Tickets cost about $12 per concert.

Solar energy was pioneered in this land of sunshine, and each year in late June the flag of sustainability is raised at the three-day **TAOS SOLAR MUSIC FESTIVAL** (www.solarmusicfest.com). Top-name acts appear, and booths promote alternative energy, permaculture, and other eco-friendly technologies.

WHERE TO STAY

The hotels and motels along NM 68 (Paseo del Pueblo Sur and Norte) suit every need and budget; rates vary little between big-name chains and smaller establishments. Make advance reservations and expect higher rates during the ski season (usually from late December to early April) and in the summer. Skiers have many choices for overnighting, from accommodations in the town of Taos to spots snuggled up right beside the slopes.

The best deals in town are the bed-and-breakfasts. Mostly family-owned, they provide personal service, delicious breakfasts, and many extras that hotels charge for. The B&Bs are often in old adobes that have been refurbished with style and flair.

DOWNTOWN TAOS

$$$$ **TOUCHSTONE INN.** D. H. Lawrence visited this house when
★ Miriam DeWitt owned it in 1929. The inn's owner, Taos artist Bren Price, has filled the rooms, named after famous Taos literary figures, with tasteful antique and modern pieces. The grounds overlook part of the Taos Pueblo lands, and this makes for a quiet stay within a mile of Taos Plaza. Some suites have fireplaces. Early morning coffee is poured in the living room, and breakfasts with inventive presentations are served in the glassed-in patio. *110 Mabel Dodge La. (Box 1885, 87571), tel. 505/758–0192 or 800/758–0192, fax 505/758–3498, www.touchstoneinn.com. 8 suites. In-room VCRs, hot tub. MC, V. BP.*

taos lodging

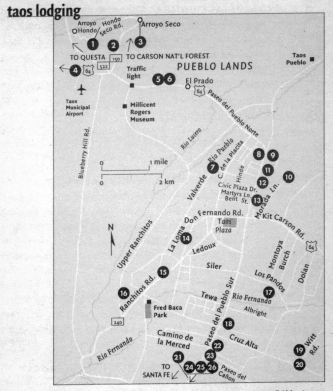

$$$–$$$$ CASA DE LAS CHIMENEAS. Tile hearths, French doors, and
★ traditional viga ceilings grace the House of Chimneys B&B, 2½
blocks from the Plaza and secluded behind thick walls. Each
room in the 1912 structure has a private entrance, a fireplace,
handmade New Mexican furniture, and a bar stocked with
complimentary beverages. All rooms overlook the gardens. Two-
course breakfasts are served, and late-afternoon hors d'oeuvres
are generous enough to be a light meal. 405 Cordoba Rd. (Box
5303, 87571), tel. 505/758–4777 or 877/758–4777, fax 505/758–3976,
www.visittaos.com. 8 rooms, 2 suites. Minibars, in-room VCRs, outdoor
hot tub, gym, sauna, laundry service; no smoking. AE, MC, V. BP.

$$$–$$$$ INN ON LA LOMA PLAZA. The walls surrounding this Pueblo
★ Revival building date from the early 1800s; the inn itself is listed
on the National Register of Historic Places. The rooms have kiva
fireplaces and Mexican-tile bathrooms; the living room has a
well-stocked library with books on Taos and art. Owners Jerry
and Peggy Davis provide helpful advice about the area and serve
a generous breakfast, afternoon snacks, and evening coffee.
Guests have privileges at the nearby health club (but there's an
outdoor hot tub here too). 315 Ranchitos Rd. (Box 4159, 87571),
tel. 505/758–1717 or 800/530–3040, fax 505/751–0155, www.
vacationtaos.com. 5 rooms, 2 studios. Some kitchenettes, hot tub, library.
AE, D, MC, V. BP.

$$–$$$$ HACIENDA DEL SOL. Art patron Mabel Dodge Luhan bought this
★ house in the 1920s and lived here with her husband, Tony Luhan,
while building their main house. It was also their private retreat
and guest house for visiting notables; Frank Waters wrote *People
of the Valley* here. Most of the rooms contain kiva fireplaces,
southwestern handcrafted furniture, and original artwork. The
secluded outdoor hot tub has a stunning view of Taos Mountain.
Breakfast is a gourmet affair. 109 Mabel Dodge La. (Box 177, 87571),
tel. 505/758–0287, fax 505/758–5895, www.taoshaciendadelsol.com.
11 rooms. Outdoor hot tub. MC, V. BP.

$$$ EARTHSHIP RENTALS. "Earthships" are passive solar homes, built partly underground, that exist "off the grid," with self-sustaining energy, water, and waste systems. Three of these uniquely charming structures are available, by the night or week, on the mesa northwest of Taos, so you can experience for yourself the home of the future. *Solar Survival, Box 1041, 87571, tel. 505/751–0462, fax 505/751–1005, www.earthship.org. 3 houses. Kitchens; no room phones, no TV in some rooms. AE, MC, V.*

$$$ RAMADA INN DE TAOS. More Taos than Ramada, the two-story adobe-style hotel welcomes you with a lobby fireplace, desert colors, western art, and Native American pottery. The rooms have an inviting southwestern flavor; some have fireplaces. *615 Paseo del Pueblo Sur, 87571, tel. 505/758–2900 or 800/659–8267, fax 505/758–1662. 124 rooms. Dining room, indoor pool, hot tub, lounge, meeting rooms. AE, D, DC, MC, V.*

$$–$$$ FECHIN INN. This graceful Pueblo Revival structure on the grounds
★ of the Fechin Institute (to which guests have free admission) is adjacent to Kit Carson Memorial Park. Painter Nicolai Fechin's daughter, Eya, participated in the planning; Fechin reproductions adorn the rooms, and the woodwork in the lobby is based on the artist's designs. Breakfast is available, as are cocktails in the evening. Rooms are comfortable, if nondescript; most have private balconies or patios. Pets are welcome and ski storage is available. *227 Paseo del Pueblo Norte, 87571, tel. 505/751–1000 or 800/811–2933, fax 505/751–7338, www.fechin–inn.com. 71 rooms, 14 suites. Gym, massage, meeting rooms. AE, D, DC, MC, V. CP.*

$$–$$$ MABEL DODGE LUHAN HOUSE. This National Historic Landmark was once the home of the heiress who drew the literati to the area. Guests included D. H. Lawrence, Georgia O'Keeffe, and Willa Cather. The main house, which has kept its simple, rustic feel, has nine guest rooms; there are eight more in a modern building, as well as a two-bedroom cottage. You can sleep in Mabel's own hand-carved bed or stay in the O'Keeffe Room or Ansel Adams Room. The inn is frequently used for artistic, cultural, and educational workshops. 240 Morada La. (Box 558, 87571), tel. 505/751–9686 or 800/846–2235, fax 505/737–0365, www.mabeldodgeluhan.com. 15 rooms, 2 with shared bath; 1 cottage. Meeting rooms. AE, MC, V. BP.

$$–$$$ **LA POSADA DE TAOS.** A couple of blocks from Taos Plaza, this provincial adobe has beam ceilings, a portal, and the intimacy of a private hacienda. Five guest rooms are in the main house; the sixth is a separate cottage with a queen-size four-poster bed, a sitting room, and a fireplace. The rooms have mountain views or face a flowering courtyard; all but one of the rooms have adobe, kiva-style fireplaces. Breakfasts are hearty. 309 Juanita La. (Box 1118, 87571), tel. 505/758–8164 or 800/645–4803, fax 505/751–4694, www.laposadadetaos.com. 5 rooms, 1 cottage. Some in-room hot tubs, hot tub. AE, MC, V. BP.

$$–$$$ **ORINDA.** Built in 1947, this adobe estate has spectacular views and country privacy. The one- and two-bedroom suites have separate entrances, kiva-style fireplaces, traditional viga ceilings, and Mexican-tile baths. Two rooms share a common sitting room. One suite has a Jacuzzi. The hearty breakfast is served family-style in the soaring two-story sun atrium amid a gallery of artworks, all for sale. 461 Valverde (Box 4451, 87571), tel. 505/758–8581 or 800/847–1837, fax 505/751–4895, www.orindabb.com. 5 suites. Some in-room hot tubs; no smoking. AE, MC, V. BP.

$$–$$$ **SAGEBRUSH INN.** A tad run-down but still charming, this Pueblo Mission–style 1929 adobe 3 mi south of the Plaza contains authentic Navajo rugs, rare pottery, southwestern and Spanish antiques, and paintings by southwestern masters. Georgia O'Keeffe once lived and painted in one of the third-story rooms. Many of the bedrooms have kiva-style fireplaces; some have balconies looking out to the Sangre de Cristo Mountains. There's country-western music nightly. The Sagebrush Village offers condominium family lodging, too. 1508 Paseo del Pueblo Sur (Box 557, 87571), tel. 505/758–2254 or 800/428–3626, fax 505/758–5077, www.sagebrushinn.com. 68 rooms, 32 suites. 2 restaurants, in-room data ports, pool, 2 hot tubs, bar, lounge, meeting rooms. AE, D, DC, MC, V.

$$–$$$ **SAN GERONIMO LODGE.** On a small street off Kit Carson Road, this lodge built in 1925 sits on 2½ acres that front majestic Taos Mountain and back up to the Carson National Forest. A balcony library, attractive grounds, many rooms with fireplaces, two rooms designed for people with disabilities, and a room for guests with a pet are among the draws. A full breakfast is served, and the hotel staff will arrange ski packages. *1101 Witt Rd., 87571, tel. 505/751–3776 or 800/894–4119, fax 505/751–1493, www. sangeronimolodge.com. 18 rooms. Pool, hot tub, massage, some pets allowed. AE, D, DC, MC, V.*

$–$$$ **SUN GOD LODGE.** Though inexpensive, this motel has old adobe charm with basic amenities; some rooms have kitchenettes and fireplaces. Right on the main highway, the Sun God is convenient to restaurants and historic sites. *919 Paseo del Pueblo Sur, 87571, tel. 505/758–3162 or 800/821–2437, fax 505/758–1716, www. sungodlodge.com. 55 rooms. Hot tub, laundry room. AE, D, MC, V.*

$$ **BEST WESTERN KACHINA LODGE DE TAOS.** Just north of Taos Plaza, this two-story Pueblo-style adobe carries the theme of the katsina (a figure representing a masked ancestral spirit) throughout. Guest rooms sustain the Native American motif, with handmade and hand-painted furnishings and colorful bedspreads. From Memorial Day to Labor Day a troupe from Taos Pueblo performs nightly ritual dances outside by firelight. *413 Paseo del Pueblo Norte (Box NN, 87571), tel. 505/758–2275 or 800/522–4462, fax 505/758–9207, www.kachinalodge.com. 113 rooms, 5 suites. Restaurant, coffee shop, pool, hot tub, bar, shops, meeting rooms. AE, D, DC, MC, V.*

$$ **BROOKS STREET INN.** An elaborately carved corbel arch, the handiwork of Japanese carpenter Yaichikido, spans the entrance to a shaded, walled garden. Fluffy pillows, fresh flowers, and paintings by local artists are among the grace notes in the rooms; some have fireplaces. Blue-corn pancakes with pineapple salsa, stuffed French toast with an apricot glaze, and other home-baked delights are served at breakfast. *119 Brooks St. (Box 4954, 87571),* tel. 505/758–1489 or 800/758–1489, www.brooksstreetinn.com. 6 rooms. No smoking. AE, MC, V. BP.

$$ CASA EUROPA. This 17th-century estate on 6 acres, with views of pastures and mountains, is furnished with European antiques and southwestern pieces. The two main guest areas are light and airy, with comfortable chairs to relax in while the fireplace crackles. Breakfasts are elaborate, and complimentary homemade afternoon pastries are served, except during ski season, when they're replaced by evening hors d'oeuvres. 840 Upper Ranchitos Rd. (HC 68, Box 3F, 87571), tel. 888/758–9798, tel./fax 505/758–9798, www.casaeuropa.com. 5 rooms, 2 suites. Hot tub, sauna, 2 lounges. AE, MC, V. BP.

$$ EL PUEBLO LODGE. This low-to-the-ground, Pueblo-style adobe a few blocks north of Taos Plaza has practical in-room amenities and guest laundry rooms. The traditional southwestern furnishings and fireplaces in some rooms lend a homey feel. 412 Paseo del Pueblo Norte (Box 92, 87571), tel. 505/758–8700 or 800/433–9612, fax 505/758–7321, www.elpueblolodge.com. 61 rooms. Some kitchenettes, refrigerators, pool, hot tub, laundry facilities. AE, D, MC, V. CP.

$$ HISTORIC TAOS INN. Mere steps from Taos Plaza, this hotel is listed on the National Register of Historic Places. The guest rooms are pleasant and comfortable, and in summer there's dining alfresco on the patio. The lobby, which also serves as seating for the Adobe Bar, is built around an old town well from which a fountain bubbles forth. Many shops and eateries are within walking distance of the inn, and its own restaurant, Doc Martin's, is quite popular itself. 125 Paseo del Pueblo Norte, 87571, tel. 505/758–2233 or 800/826–7466, fax 505/758–5776, www.taosinn.com. 36 rooms. Restaurant, bar, lounge, library. AE, DC, MC, V.

$$ HOLIDAY INN DON FERNANDO DE TAOS. The accommodations at this hotel with a Pueblo-style design are grouped around central courtyards and connected by walkways. Appointed with hand-carved New Mexican furnishings, some rooms have kiva-style fireplaces. There's a free shuttle to take guests to the town center. *1005 Paseo del Pueblo Sur, 87571, tel. 505/758–4444 or 800/759–2736, fax 505/758–0055, www.holiday-taos.com. 124 rooms. Restaurant, in-room data ports, some refrigerators, tennis court, indoor pool, hot tub, bar, lounge. AE, D, DC, MC, V.*

$$ **OLD TAOS GUESTHOUSE.** Once a ramshackle adobe hacienda, this homey B&B has been completely and lovingly outfitted with the owners' hand-carved doors and furniture, western artifacts, and antiques. Some rooms have the smallest bathrooms you'll ever encounter but have private entrances, and some have fireplaces. There are 80-mi views from the outdoor hot tub, and it's just a five-minute drive to town. The owners welcome families. Breakfasts are healthy and hearty. *1028 Witt Rd. (Box 6552, 87571), tel. 800/758–5448, tel./fax 505/758–5448, www.oldtaos.com. 9 rooms. Hot tub. MC, V. BP.*

RANCHOS DE TAOS

$$–$$$$ **ADOBE & PINES INN.** Native American and Mexican artifacts decorate the main house of this B&B, which has expansive mountain views. Part of the main building dates from 1830. The rooms contain Mexican-tiled baths, kiva fireplaces, fluffy goose-down pillows, and comforters. A separate cottage and two equally handsome casitas also house guests. The owners serve gourmet breakfasts in a sunny glass-enclosed patio. *NM 68 and Llano Quemado (Box 837, Ranchos de Taos 87557), tel. 505/751–0947 or 800/723–8267, fax 505/758–8423, www.adobepines.com. 5 rooms, 1 cottage, 2 casitas. 5 hot tubs, sauna; no smoking. AE, MC, V. BP.*

ARROYO SECO

$$$–$$$$ **ALMA DEL MONTE.** Mountain views abound from the rooms and the courtyard of this B&B on the high plain between Taos and the ski valley. Heated saltillo-tiled floors, kiva fireplaces, whirlpool baths, Victorian antiques, generous breakfasts, and afternoon wine with hors d'oeuvres make it a hard place to leave, even for skiing.

Children must be 16 or older. *372 Hondo Seco Rd. (Box 1434, Taos 87571), tel. 505/776–2721 or 800/273–7203, fax 505/776–8888, www.almaspirit.com. 5 rooms. In-room hot tubs, hot tub. MC, V. BP.*

$$–$$$$ **CASA GRANDE GUEST RANCH.** Watch the stars and the lights of Taos twinkle as you soak in the hot tub of this B&B; morning views stretch for miles. Three comfortable rooms are integrated into the family home built not far from the property's historic hacienda on the flanks of El Salto Mountain. Breakfast burritos with all the trimmings will see you through a horseback ride up to the waterfalls. Children must be 18 and over. *75 Luis O. Torres Rd., Arroyo Seco 87514, tel. 888/236–1303, fax 505/776–2177, www. guestranch.com. 3 rooms. Hot tub. AE, MC, V. BP.*

$$–$$$$ **QUAIL RIDGE INN RESORT.** On the way to Taos Ski Valley, this large resort has one- and two-story modern adobe bungalows that are comfy and efficient. Some suites have kitchens; all have fireplaces. The resort provides a host of recreational amenities, from organized trail rides to hot-tub soaks. Skiing, tennis, rafting, mountain-biking, and fly-fishing packages are available for groups or individuals. *Taos Ski Valley Rd. (C.R. 150; Box 707, Taos 87571), tel. 505/776–2211 or 800/624–4448, fax 505/776–2949, www. taoswebb.com/hotel/quailridge. 50 rooms, 60 suites. Restaurant, in-room data ports, 8 tennis courts, pool, gym, hot tub, racquetball, squash, volleyball, lounge, meeting rooms. AE, D, DC, MC, V.*

CAMPING

CARSON NATIONAL FOREST. Within the forest are dozens of campsites along 400 mi of cool mountain trout streams and lakes. You may also choose your own site, anywhere along a forest road. Rest rooms are provided. Contact the U.S. Forest Service for the latest camping information. *Forest Service Building, 208 Cruz Alta Rd., Taos 87571, tel. 505/758–6200. Free–$7.*

ORILLA VERDE RECREATION AREA. You can hike, fish, and picnic at this area along the banks of the Rio Grande, 10 mi south of Ranchos de Taos, off NM 68 at NM 570. As for paying the camping fee, leave cash in an envelope provided, drop it in a tube, and the rangers will collect it. *Bureau of Land Management, Cruz Alta Rd., Taos 87571, tel. 505/758–8851. Flush toilets, drinking water, fire grates, picnic tables. 70 tent sites. $10. No credit cards. Closed mid-Oct.–Apr.*

QUESTA LODGE. This RV park is on the Red River off the Enchanted Circle, just off NM 522. There are areas for basketball, croquet, and volleyball. *Lower Embargo Rd. (Box 155, Questa 87556), tel. 505/586–0300. Flush toilets, drinking water, laundry facilities, showers, fire grates, picnic tables, playground. 26 RV sites. $20. Closed mid-Oct.–Mar.*

TAOS RV PARK. The sites are grassy, with a few small trees, in this park 3½ mi from Taos Plaza near the junction of NM 68 and NM 518. A recreation room has video games, TV, and a pool table. Some RV supplies are for sale. There are horseshoes, billiards, and a kitchen area. *1800 Paseo del Pueblo Sur, next to the Budget Host Inn (Box 729F, Ranchos de Taos 87557), tel. 505/758–2524 or 800/323–6009, www.newmex.com/rv. Flush toilets, full hook-ups, drinking water, showers, picnic tables, electricity, public telephone, general store, playground. 62 RV sites, 28 tent sites. RV sites $24–$27, tent sites $18. D, MC, V.*

practical information

Air Travel

Most major airlines provide service to the state's main airport in Albuquerque, about an hour's drive from Santa Fe. There is no air service between Albuquerque and Santa Fe. Rio Grande Air operates daily flights between Albuquerque and Taos. Great Lakes Aviation flies daily from Denver to Santa Fe; round-trip fares are usually around $250.

➤MAJOR AIRLINES: **America West** (tel. 800/235–9292). **American** (tel. 800/433–7300). **Continental** (tel. 800/525–0280). **Delta** (tel. 800/221–1212). **Northwest** (tel. 800/692–7000). **Southwest Airlines** (tel. 800/435–9792). **TWA** (tel. 800/221–2000). **United** (tel. 800/241–6522). **US Airways** (tel. 800/428–4322).

➤SMALLER AIRLINES: **Frontier** (tel. 800/432–1359). **Great Lakes Aviation** (tel. 800/554–5111). **Mesa Airlines** (tel. 800/637–2247). **Rio Grande Air** (tel. 877/435–9742).

➤FROM THE U.K.: **British Airways** (tel. 0345/222–111). **Delta** (tel. 0800/414–767). **United Airlines** (tel. 0800/888–555).

CUTTING COSTS

The least expensive airfares to New Mexico usually must be purchased in advance and are nonrefundable. Albuquerque has relatively few direct flights to other parts of the country, and virtually none to the Northeast. Because the discount airline Southwest serves Albuquerque, fares from here to airports served by Southwest are often 25% to 35% less than to other airports. For instance, it's almost always cheaper to fly from Hartford, Providence, or Baltimore to Albuquerque than from Boston, New York, or Washington. It's smart to **call a number of airlines**, and when you are quoted a good price, **book it on the spot**—the same fare may not be available the next day. Always **check different routings** and look into using alternate airports. Also, price off-peak flights, which may be significantly less expensive than others. Travel agents, especially low-fare specialists (☞ Discounts and Deals, *below*), are helpful.

Consolidators are another good source. They buy tickets for scheduled international flights at reduced rates from the airlines, then sell them at prices that beat the best fare available directly from the airlines. Sometimes you can even get your money back if you need to return the ticket. Carefully read the fine print detailing penalties for changes and cancellations, purchase the ticket with a credit card, and **confirm your consolidator reservation with the airline.**

➤CONSOLIDATORS: **Cheap Tickets** (tel. 800/377–1000 or 888/922–8849, www.cheaptickets.com). **Discount Airline Ticket Service** (tel. 800/576–1600). **Unitravel** (tel. 800/325–2222, www.unitravel.com). **Up & Away Travel** (tel. 212/889–2345, www.upandaway.com). **World Travel Network** (tel. 800/409–6753).

HOW TO COMPLAIN

If your baggage goes astray or your flight goes awry, complain right away. Most carriers require that you **file a claim immediately.** The Aviation Consumer Protection Division of the Department of Transportation publishes *Fly-Rights*, which discusses airlines and consumer issues and is available on-line. At PassengerRights.com, a Web site, you can compose a letter of complaint and distribute it electronically.

➤AIRLINE COMPLAINTS: **Aviation Consumer Protection Division** (U.S. Department of Transportation, Room 4107,

C-75, Washington, DC 20590, tel. 202/366–2220, www. dot.gov/airconsumer). **Federal Aviation Administration Consumer Hotline** (tel. 800/322–7873).

Airports

The major gateway to New Mexico is Albuquerque International Sunport, which is 65 mi southwest of Santa Fe and 130 mi south of Taos. Some travelers to Taos prefer to fly into Denver (four to five hours' drive), which has far more direct flights to the rest of the country than Albuquerque—it's a scenic drive, too.

➤AIRPORT INFORMATION: **Albuquerque International Sunport** (Sunport Blvd. off I–25, 5 mi south of downtown, tel. 505/244–7700, www.cabq.gov/airport). **Denver International Airport** (8500 Peña Blvd., off I–70, Exit 285, tel. 303/342–2000, www.flydenver.com). **Santa Fe Municipal Airport** (Airport Rd. off NM 284, 10 mi southwest of downtown, tel. 505/955–2908). **Taos Municipal Airport** (U.S. 64, 12 mi west of Taos, tel. 505/ 758–4995).

AIRPORT TRANSFERS

Shuttle buses between the Albuquerque International Sunport and Santa Fe take about 1 hour and 20 minutes and cost approximately $20–$25 each way. Shuttle service runs from Albuquerque to Taos and nearby ski areas; the ride takes 2¾ to 3 hours and costs $35–$50. Greyhound bus service costs considerably less than those charged by the shuttle services listed here.

➤BETWEEN ALBUQUERQUE AND SANTA FE: **Gray Line/Coach USA** (tel. 800/256–8991). **Sandia Shuttle Express** (tel. 505/474–5696 or 888/775–5696, www.sandiashuttle. com). **Santa Fe Shuttle** (tel. 505/243–2300 or 888/833–2300, www.santafeshuttle.com).

➤BETWEEN ALBUQUERQUE AND TAOS: **Faust's Transportation** (tel. 505/758–7359 or 888/830–3410, www.

newmexiconet.com/faust1.htm). **Pride of Taos** (tel. 505/758–8340 or 800/273–8340). **Twin Hearts Express** (tel. 505/751–1201 or 800/654–9456).

Business Hours

Banks generally are open 9 to 3 or 4 on weekdays and 9 or 10 to noon on Saturday. Post offices are open from 8 or 9 until 5 on weekdays and until noon on Saturday. There is only one all-night pharmacy in Santa Fe (☞ Emergencies, *below*), none in Taos. Museums usually are open daily from 9 or 10 AM to 5 or 6 PM, although hours may vary seasonally. Many are closed on Monday. Some are open for extended hours on Friday evening. Some pueblos are closed to visitors for short periods throughout the year.

Bus Travel

Bus service to Santa Fe and Taos is available via Texas, New Mexico & Oklahoma Coaches, affiliated with Greyhound Lines.

➤BUS INFORMATION: **Greyhound/Texas, New Mexico & Oklahoma Coaches** (tel. 505/243–4435 or 800/231–2222). **Las Cruces Shuttle Service** (tel. 505/525–1784 or 800/288–1784, www.lascrucesshuttle.com).

➤BUS STATIONS: **Taos Bus Station** (1008 Paseo del Pueblo Sur, tel. 505/758–1144).

WITHIN SANTA FE

The city's bus system, Santa Fe Trails, is useful for getting from the Plaza to some of the outlying attractions. Route 10 runs from downtown to the museums on Old Santa Fe Trail south of town. A daily pass costs $1. Buses run 6 AM to 10 PM about every 30 minutes on weekdays, and every hour until 8 PM on Saturday. There is no bus service on Sunday.

➤BUS SERVICE: **Santa Fe Trails** (tel. 505/438–1464).

WITHIN TAOS

The Taos transit department's Chile Line bus service has two lines. The Green Line circles around town, while the Red Line runs between Taos Pueblo and the Ranchos de Taos post office. Tickets are 50¢, all-day passes $1.

➤BUS INFORMATION: **Chile Line** (tel. 505/751–4459).

Cameras and Photography

New Mexico's wildlife and rugged landscape are extremely photogenic. The striking red sandstone cliffs and soil of northern New Mexico make a terrific backdrop. **Check the rules on Indian reservations** before you take photographs there. In many cases, you must purchase a permit. Restrictions can range from no built-in telephoto lenses to no photography altogether. Be sure you have permission to photograph any Native American you encounter, since beliefs regarding this practice vary. Additionally, your actions might be interpreted as downright rude.

The *Kodak Guide to Shooting Great Travel Pictures* (available at bookstores everywhere) is loaded with tips.

➤PHOTO HELP: **Kodak Information Center** (tel. 800/242–2424, www.kodak.com).

EQUIPMENT PRECAUTIONS

Don't pack film and equipment in checked luggage, where it is much more susceptible to damage. X-ray machines used to view checked luggage are becoming much more powerful and therefore are much more likely to ruin your film. Try to **ask for hand inspection of film,** which becomes clouded after repeated exposure to airport X-ray machines, and **keep videotapes and computer disks away from metal detectors.** Always **keep film, tape, and computer disks out of the sun.** Carry an extra supply of batteries, and **be prepared to turn on your camera, camcorder, or laptop** to prove to airport security personnel that the device is real.

In New Mexico, dust can be a problem. Keep cameras and video equipment in cases while not in use. Also, keep in mind that extreme heat can ruin film. Don't leave your equipment in a hot car or under direct sunlight.

Car Rental

A typical rate is about $28 to $35 daily and $160 to $200 weekly for an economy car with air-conditioning, automatic transmission, and unlimited mileage. Most agencies won't rent to people under the age of 21.

➤MAJOR AGENCIES: Alamo (tel. 800/327–9633, www.alamo. com). Avis (tel. 800/331–1212; 800/879–2847 in Canada; 02/9353–9000 in Australia; 09/526–2847 in New Zealand; 0870/606–0100 in the U.K.; www.avis.com). Budget (tel. 800/527–0700; 0870/156–5656 in the U.K.; www.budget.com). Dollar (tel. 800/800–4000; 0124/622–0111 in the U.K., where it's affiliated with Sixt; 02/9223–1444 in Australia; www.dollar. com). Hertz (tel. 800/654–3131; 800/263–0600 in Canada; 020/8897–2072 in the U.K.; 02/9669–2444 in Australia; 09/256–8690 in New Zealand; www.hertz.com). National Car Rental (tel. 800/227–7368; 020/8680–4800 in the U.K.; www. nationalcar.com).

➤LOCAL AGENCIES: Cottam Walker (1320 Paseo del Pueblo Sur, Taos, tel. 505/751–3200). Dollar Rent a Car (Taos Municipal Airport, tel. 505/751–1000).

CUTTING COSTS

For a good deal, book through a travel agent, who will shop around. Also, price local car-rental companies—whose prices may be lower still, although their service and maintenance may not be as good as those of major rental agencies—and research rates on-line. Remember to ask about required deposits, cancellation penalties, and drop-off charges if you're planning to pick up the car in one city and leave it in another. If you're traveling during a holiday period, also make sure that a confirmed reservation guarantees you a car.

INSURANCE

For about $15 to $20 a day, rental companies sell protection, known as a collision- or loss-damage waiver (CDW or LDW), that eliminates your liability for damage to the car; it's always optional and should never be automatically added to your bill. In most states you don't need a CDW if you have personal auto insurance or other liability insurance. However, **make sure you have enough coverage to pay for the car.**

SURCHARGES

Before you pick up a car in one city and leave it in another, **ask about drop-off charges or one-way service fees,** which can be substantial. Note, too, that some rental agencies charge extra if you return the car before the time specified in your contract. To avoid a hefty refueling fee, **fill the tank just before you turn in the car,** but be aware that gas stations near the rental outlet may overcharge. It's almost never a deal to buy the tank of gas in the car when you rent it; the understanding is that you'll return it empty, but some fuel usually remains. Surcharges may apply if you're under 25. You'll pay extra for child seats (about $6 a day), which are compulsory for children under five, and for additional drivers (about $5 per day).

Car Travel

A car is a necessity in Santa Fe and Taos, as public transportation is minimal. Roads on Native American lands are designated by wooden, arrow-shape signs and you'd best adhere to the speed limit; some roads on reservation or forest land aren't paved. Even in the cities, quite a few surface streets are unpaved and often bumpy and narrow—Santa Fe, for instance, has a higher percentage of dirt roads than any other state capital in the nation.

South–north–running I–25 actually curves in almost a west–east direction as it cuts just south of Santa Fe, which is 62 mi northeast of Albuquerque. U.S. 285/84 runs north–south through the city. The Turquoise Trail is a scenic, two-lane approach to Santa Fe from Albuquerque. The NM 599 bypass, also called the Santa Fe Relief Route, cuts around the city from I–25's Exit 276, southwest of the city, to U.S. 285/84, north of the city; it's a great shortcut if you're heading from Albuquerque to Española, Abiquiu, Taos, or other points north of Santa Fe.

The main route from Santa Fe to Taos is NM 68, also known as the Low Road, which winds between the Rio Grande and red-rock cliffs before rising to a spectacular view of the plain and river gorge. You can also take the wooded High Road to Taos (☞ Side Trips from Santa Fe). The altitude in Taos will affect your car's performance, causing it to "gasp" because it's getting too much gas and not enough air. If a smooth ride matters, you can have your car tuned up for high-altitude driving.

EMERGENCY SERVICES

Depending on the location, either the New Mexico State Police or the county sheriff's department responds to road emergencies. Call the city or village police department if you encounter trouble within the limits of a municipality. Indian reservations have tribal police headquarters, and rangers assist travelers within U.S. Forest Service boundaries.

GASOLINE

There's a lot of high, dry, lonesome country in New Mexico—it's possible to go 50 or 60 mi in some of the less-populated areas between gas stations. For a safe trip **keep your gas tank full.** Self-service gas stations are the norm in New Mexico, though in some of the less populated regions you'll find stations with full service. At press time, the cost of unleaded gas at self-service stations was about $1.10 per gallon in most of the state and $1.25 to $1.40 in Santa Fe and Taos.

PARKING

Parking in Santa Fe is difficult, but public and private lots can be found throughout the city. There are parking garages near the Plaza on San Francisco and Water streets. On weekends, you can park for free in the lots of some of the government buildings near the Capitol, which is within walking distance of the Plaza. In Taos, there's a metered parking lot between Taos Plaza and Bent Street and a free lot on Kit Carson, two blocks east of Paseo del Pueblo.

ROAD CONDITIONS

Arroyos (dry washes or gullies) are bridged on major roads, but lesser roads often dip down through them. These can be a hazard during the rainy season, July–early September. Even if it looks shallow, **don't try to cross an arroyo filled with water**—it may have an axle-breaking hole in the middle. Wait a little while, and it will drain off almost as quickly as it filled. If you stall in a running arroyo, get out of the car and onto high ground if possible. In the backcountry, never drive (or walk) in a dry arroyo bed if the sky is dark anywhere upstream. A sudden thunderstorm 15 mi away could send a raging flash flood down a wash in a matter of minutes.

Unless they are well graded and graveled, **avoid unpaved roads in New Mexico when they are wet.** The soil contains a lot of caliche, or clay, which gets very slick when mixed with water. During winter storms roads may be shut down entirely; call the State Highway Department for road conditions.

At certain times in fall or spring, New Mexico winds can be vicious for large vehicles like RVs. Driving conditions can be particularly treacherous in passages through foothills or mountains where wind gusts are concentrated.

New Mexico has a very high incidence of drunk driving and uninsured motorists. Factor in the state's high speed limits, many winding and steep roads, and eye-popping scenery, and you can see how important it is to drive as alertly and defensively as possible. On the plus side, major traffic jams are a rarity even in cities.

➤ROAD CONDITIONS: **State Highway Department** (tel. 800/432–4269).

ROAD MAPS

Signage is spotty in many rural areas, and relatively few communities are laid out in an easy-to-follow grid pattern; it's important to invest in a good road map if you're planning extensive exploring. You can pick up a free, detailed state map from area tourism offices or from the New Mexico Department of Tourism. GTR Mapping produces topographical maps of the state that depict backroads and recreational sites—these are available at many bookshops and convenience stores.

➤MAPS: **New Mexico Department of Tourism** (tel. 505/827–7400 or 800/733–6396 ext. 0643, www.newmexico.org). **GTR Mapping** (tel. 719/275–8948).

RULES OF THE ROAD

The speed limit along the interstates in much of New Mexico is 70 or 75 mph; it's 65 to 70 on U.S. highways (55 in more populated areas). Right-on-red turns are permitted except where signs indicate otherwise. Speed limits are strictly enforced, especially along interstates and major U.S. and state highways. Radar detectors are legal in New Mexico. The use of seat belts in the front of the car is required by law in New Mexico. Always strap children under age five into approved child-safety seats. The state has an unusually high incidence of drunken driving–related accidents, and you might encounter sobriety checkpoints. The legal adult blood-alcohol content (BAC) limit is .08.

Children in New Mexico

If you are renting a car, don't forget to **arrange for a car seat** when you reserve. For general advice about traveling with children, consult *Fodor's FYI: Travel with Your Baby* (available in bookstores everywhere).

FLYING

If your children are two or older, **ask about children's airfares.** As a general rule, infants under two not occupying a seat fly at greatly reduced fares or even for free.

Experts agree that it's a good idea to use safety seats aloft for children weighing less than 40 pounds. Airlines set their own policies: U.S. carriers usually require that the child be ticketed, even if he or she is young enough to ride free, since the seats must be strapped into regular seats. Do **check your airline's policy about using safety seats during takeoff and landing.** Safety seats are not allowed everywhere in the plane, so get your seat assignments as early as possible.

SIGHTS AND ATTRACTIONS

Places that are especially appealing to children are indicated by a rubber-duckie icon (☺) in the margin.

➤**ADVENTURE HOLIDAYS: Santa Fe Detours** (tel. 505/983-6565 or 800/338-6877, www.sfdetours.com).

Consumer Protection

Whether you're shopping for gifts or purchasing travel services, **pay with a major credit card** whenever possible, so you can cancel payment or get reimbursed if there's a problem (and you can provide documentation). If you're doing business with a particular company for the first time, **contact your local Better Business Bureau and the attorney general's offices** in your state and (for U.S. businesses) the company's home state as well. Have any complaints been filed? Finally, if you're buying a package or tour, always **consider travel insurance** that includes default coverage (☞ Insurance, *below*).

➤**BBBS: Council of Better Business Bureaus** (4200 Wilson Blvd., Suite 800, Arlington, VA 22203, tel. 703/276–0100, fax 703/525–8277, www.bbb.org). **Better Business Bureau** (2625 Pennsylvania NE, Suite 2050, Albuquerque 87110, tel. 505/884–0500; 800/873–2224 in New Mexico; fax 505/346–0696; www.bbbnm.com).

Dining

New Mexico has some of the best Mexican food in the Southwest, and ingredients and style vary even within the state. Most longtime residents like their chili (which is seasoned with red or green chile) with some fire—in the Santa Fe, Albuquerque, and Las Cruces areas, chili is sometimes celebrated for its ability to set off smoke alarms. Excellent barbecue and steaks also can be found throughout New Mexico. The restaurants we list are the cream of the crop in each price category.

CATEGORY	COST*
$$$$	over $25
$$$	$18–$25
$$	$10–$17
$	under $10

*per person for a main course at dinner

RESERVATIONS AND DRESS

Reservations are always a good idea; we mention them only when they're essential or not accepted. Book as far ahead as you can, and reconfirm as soon as you arrive. (Large parties should always call ahead to check the reservations policy.) We mention dress only when men are required to wear a jacket or a jacket and tie. Even at nicer restaurants in New Mexico, dress is usually casual.

Statewide, many kitchens stop serving around 8 PM, so **don't arrive too late** if you're looking forward to a leisurely dinner.

Disabilities and Accessibility

Most of the region's national parks and recreational areas have accessible visitor centers, rest rooms, campsites, and trails.

➤LOCAL RESOURCES: **National Park Service, Intermountain Support Office** (Box 728, Santa Fe 87504, tel. 505/988–6091).

LODGING

Despite the Americans with Disabilities Act, the definition of accessibility seems to differ from hotel to hotel. Some properties may be accessible by ADA standards for people with mobility problems but not for people with hearing or vision impairments, for example. Furthermore, many accommodations in New Mexico are historic or quite small and do not conform even to ADA mobility standards.

If you have mobility problems, ask for the lowest floor on which accessible services are offered. If you have a hearing impairment, check whether the hotel has devices to alert you visually to the ring of the telephone, knock at the door, and a fire/emergency alarm. Some hotels provide these devices without charge. Discuss your needs with hotel personnel if this equipment isn't available, so that a staff member can personally alert you in the event of an emergency. If you're bringing a guide dog, get authorization ahead of time and write down the name of the person you spoke with.

➤ACCESSIBLE ROOMS: **Hilton of Santa Fe** (tel. 505/988–2811, www.hiltonofsantafe.com).

RESERVATIONS

When discussing accessibility with an operator or reservations agent, **ask hard questions.** Are there any stairs, inside or out? Are there grab bars next to the toilet *and* in the shower/tub? How wide is the doorway to the room? To the bathroom? For the most extensive facilities meeting the latest legal specifications, **opt for newer accommodations.** If you reserve through a toll-free number, consider also calling the hotel's local number to confirm the information from the central reservations office. Get confirmation in writing when you can.

SIGHTS AND ATTRACTIONS

Santa Fe has many narrow streets and walkways and ancient buildings that can be less than convenient for wheelchairs.

➤**NEW MEXICO GUIDEBOOKS: Developmental Disabilities Planning Council** (tel. 505/827–7590). **Governor's Concerns on the Handicapped** (tel. 505/827–6465; 505/827–6329 TDD; 877/696–1470 in New Mexico; www.state.nm.us/gcch/accessnm.htm). **New Mexico Department of Tourism** (tel. 505/827–7400 or 800/733–6396 ext. 0643, www.newmexico.org/visitor/disabled.html).

TRANSPORTATION

Specially equipped vehicles can be rented from **Wheelchair Getaways of New Mexico** (Box 93501, Albuquerque 87199, tel. 505/247–2626 or 800/408–2626, www.wheelchair-getaways.com). Automatic wheelchair lifts or ramps along with hand controls are included in vans, which will be delivered to the Albuquerque International Sunport upon request.

➤**COMPLAINTS: Aviation Consumer Protection Division** (☞ Air Travel, *above*) for airline-related problems. **Departmental Office of Civil Rights** (for general inquiries, U.S. Department of Transportation, S-30, 400 7th St. SW, Room 10215, Washington, DC 20590, tel. 202/366–4648, fax 202/366–3571, www.dot.gov/ost/docr/index.htm). **Disability Rights Section** (NYAV, U.S. Department of Justice, Civil Rights Division, 950 Pennsylvania Ave. NW, Washington, DC 20530; tel. ADA information line 202/514–0301, 800/514–0301; 202/514–0383 TTY; 800/514–0383 TTY; www.usdoj.gov/crt/ada/adahom1.htm).

TRAVEL AGENCIES

In the United States, the Americans with Disabilities Act requires that travel firms serve the needs of all travelers. Some agencies specialize in working with people with disabilities.

➤**TRAVELERS WITH MOBILITY PROBLEMS: Access Adventures** (206 Chestnut Ridge Rd., Scottsville, NY 14624, tel. 716/889–9096), run by a former physical-rehabilitation counselor. **Accessible Vans of America** (9 Spielman Rd., Fairfield, NJ 07004, tel. 877/282–8267; 888/282–8267 reservations; fax 973/808–9713; www.accessiblevans.com). **Flying Wheels Travel** (143 W. Bridge St. [Box 382, Owatonna, MN 55060], tel. 507/451–5005, fax 507/451–1685, www.flyingwheelstravel.com).

Discounts and Deals

DISCOUNT RESERVATIONS

To save money, look into discount reservations services with Web sites and toll-free numbers, which use their buying power to get a better price on hotels, airline tickets, even car rentals. When booking a room, always **call the hotel's local toll-free number** (if one is available) rather than the central reservations number—you'll often get a better price. Always ask about special packages or corporate rates.

➤**AIRLINE TICKETS: tel. 800/AIR–4LESS.**

➤**HOTEL ROOMS: Hotel Reservations Network** (tel. 800/964–6835, www.hoteldiscount.com). **RMC Travel** (tel. 800/245–5738, www.rmcwebtravel.com). **Turbotrip.com** (tel. 800/473–7829, www.turbotrip.com).

Ecotourism

New Mexico has a wide variety of cactus species, which grow so abundantly that it might seem harmless to dig up a plant or two as a souvenir. Don't do it. Laws prohibit this practice, as certain species are becoming scarce. Avoid picking up lizards or related species, which also are becoming increasingly protected. It's also illegal to carry off Indian artifacts such as arrowheads or pottery from public land. On U.S. Bureau of Land Management land, it's okay to collect many types of rock samples, but clarify rules depending on the district you're visiting. Southern New Mexico has many caves open to visitors mostly by permit. If you visit a cave, don't leave any traces of yourself (pack it in, pack it out) and don't touch the delicate formations.

➤**EMERGENCIES:** In an emergency, dial 911.

➤**HOSPITAL: Holy Cross Hospital** (630 Paseo del Pueblo Sur, Taos, tel. 505/758–8883). **St. Vincent Hospital** (455 St. Michael's Dr., Santa Fe, tel. 505/983–3361).

➤**PHARMACIES: Raley's Pharmacy** (1100 Paseo del Pueblo Sur, Taos, tel. 505/758–1203). **Taos Pharmacy** (Piñon Plaza, 622A Paseo del Pueblo Sur, Taos, tel. 505/758–3342). **Wal-Mart Discount Pharmacy** (926 Paseo de Pueblo Sur, Taos, tel. 505/758–2743).**Walgreens** (1096 St. Francis Dr., Santa Fe, tel. 505/982–4643).

➤**POLICE: New Mexico state police** (tel. 505/758–8878). **Taos Police** (tel. 505/758–2216).

Etiquette and Behavior

See Reservations and Pueblos in Introducing Santa Fe and Taos for information about proper etiquette when visiting Native American lands.

Gay and Lesbian Travel

According to the 2000 U.S. Census, Santa Fe is second only to San Francisco in the percentage of households headed by same-sex couples. Taos also has very high numbers of lesbian and gay residents and visitors. Elsewhere in the state, somewhat more conservative attitudes prevail, but overall New Mexico is fairly tolerant. You'll find many romantic, gay-friendly inns and also gay-owned shops and eateries in Santa Fe and Taos, but there's very little in the way of gay nightlife. The monthly *Out! Magazine* (no relation to the national magazine *Out*) provides coverage of

New Mexico. A chapter in *Fodor's Gay Guide to the USA* (available at bookstores everywhere) covers Santa Fe, Taos, Albuquerque, and El Paso, Texas.

➤RESOURCES: *Out! Magazine* (tel. 505/243–2540, www.outmagazine.com).

➤GAY- AND LESBIAN-FRIENDLY TRAVEL AGENCIES: **Different Roads Travel** (8383 Wilshire Blvd., Suite 902, Beverly Hills, CA 90211, tel. 323/651–5557 or 800/429–8747, fax 323/651–3678). **Kennedy Travel** (314 Jericho Turnpike, Floral Park, NY 11001, tel. 516/352–4888 or 800/237–7433, fax 516/354–8849, www.kennedytravel.com). **Now, Voyager** (4406 18th St., San Francisco, CA 94114, tel. 415/626–1169 or 800/255–6951, fax 415/626–8626, www.nowvoyager.com). **Skylink Travel and Tour** (1006 Mendocino Ave., Santa Rosa, CA 95401, tel. 707/546–9888 or 800/225–5759, fax 707/546–9891), serving lesbian travelers.

Insurance

The most useful travel-insurance plan is a comprehensive policy that includes coverage for trip cancellation and interruption, default, trip delay, and medical expenses (with a waiver for pre-existing conditions). Without insurance you will lose all or most of your money if you cancel your trip, regardless of the reason. Default insurance covers you if your tour operator, airline, or cruise line goes out of business. Trip-delay covers expenses that arise because of bad weather or mechanical delays. Study the fine print when comparing policies.

Always buy travel policies directly from the insurance company; if you buy them from a cruise line, airline, or tour operator that goes out of business you probably will not be covered for the agency or operator's default, a major risk. Before making any purchase, **review your existing health and home-owner's policies** to find what they cover away from home.

►**TRAVEL INSURERS: In the United States: Access America** (6600 W. Broad St., Richmond, VA 23230, tel. 800/284–8300, fax 804/673–1491 or 800/346–9265, www.accessamerica. com). **Travel Guard International** (1145 Clark St., Stevens Point, WI 54481, tel. 715/345–0505 or 800/826–1300, fax 800/ 955–8785, www.travelguard.com).

Lodging

The lodgings we list are the cream of the crop in each price category. We always list the facilities that are available—but we don't specify whether they cost extra: when pricing accommodations, always ask what's included and what costs extra. Rates are highest during the peak tourist months of July and August and during Christmas and winter ski season. Off-season rates, which fluctuate, tend to be 20% lower than peak rates. Several organizations can help you find accommodations in and around Santa Fe and Taos.

CATEGORY	GREATER SANTA FE*	TAOS AND ELSEWHERE*
$$$$	over $220	over $170
$$$	$160–$220	$120–$170
$$	$100–$160	$70–$120
$	under $100	under $70

All prices are for a standard double room, excluding tax (5.6%–7%), in peak season.

Assume that hotels operate on the **European Plan** (EP, with no meals) unless we specify that they use the **Continental Plan** (CP, with a Continental breakfast), **Breakfast Plan** (BP, with a full breakfast), **Modified American Plan** (MAP, with breakfast and dinner), or the **Full American Plan** (FAP, with all meals).

►**RESERVATIONS: New Mexico Central Reservations** (tel. 800/ 466–7829, www.nmtravel.com). **Taos Central Reservations** (Box 1713, Taos 87571, tel. 505/758–9767 or 800/821–2437, www.taoscentralreservations.com). **Taos Lodging** (Box 1101,

Taos 87571, tel. 505/751–1771 or 800/954–8267, www.taoslodging.com). **Taos Ski Central** (Box 696, Village of Taos Ski Valley 87525, tel. 800/238–2829, www.taosskicentral.com). **Traditional Taos Inns Association** (tel. 505/776–8840, www.taos.lodging.com).

APARTMENT AND VILLA RENTALS

If you want a home base that's roomy enough for a family and comes with cooking facilities, consider a furnished rental. These can save you money, especially if you're traveling with a group. Vacation home, condo, and cabin rentals are numerous in Taos and Santa Fe. Management companies include Taos Vacation Rentals in Taos and the Management Group in Santa Fe.

➤MANAGEMENT COMPANIES: **The Management Group** (tel. 505/982–2823, www.santafe-rentals.com). **Santa Fe Vacation Rental** (tel. 888/340–2883, www.staabvr.com). **Southwestern Exclusives** (tel. 505/995–0777 or 800/358–8133, www.southwesternexclusives.com). **Taos Vacation Rentals** (tel. 800/788–8267, www.taosvacationrentals.com).

BED-AND-BREAKFASTS

B&Bs in New Mexico run the gamut from rooms in locals' homes to grandly restored adobe or Victorian homes.

➤RESERVATION SERVICES: **Bed and Breakfast of New Mexico** (tel. 505/982–3332, www.santafebnb.com). **New Mexico Bed and Breakfast Association** (tel. 505/766–5380 or 800/661–6649, www.nmbba.org).

HOME EXCHANGES

If you would like to exchange your home for someone else's, join a home-exchange organization, which will send you its updated listings of available exchanges for a year and will include your own listing in at least one of them. It's up to you to make specific arrangements.

➤**EXCHANGE CLUBS: HomeLink International** (Box 47747, Tampa, FL 33647, tel. 813/975–9825 or 800/638–3841, fax 813/910–8144, www.homelink.org; $106 per year). **Intervac U.S.** (30 Corte San Fernando, Tiburon, CA 94920, tel. 800/756–4663, fax 415/435–7440, www.intervacus.com; $90 yearly fee for a listing, on-line access, and a catalog; $50 without catalog).

HOTELS

Premium hotel rooms in the state capital of Santa Fe tend to fill up during sessions of the New Mexico Legislature, typically conducted during the first three months of the year. Summer weekends can pack hotel rooms in Taos, so make sure you have reservations in advance. All hotels listed have private bath unless otherwise noted.

➤**TOLL-FREE NUMBERS: Best Western** (tel. 800/528–1234, www.bestwestern.com). **Choice** (tel. 800/221–2222, www.choicehotels.com). **Clarion** (tel. 800/252–7466, www.choicehotels.com). **Comfort Inn** (tel. 800/228–5150, www.choicehotels.com). **Days Inn** (tel. 800/325–2525, www.daysinn.com). **Doubletree and Red Lion Hotels** (tel. 800/222–8733, www.hilton.com). **Embassy Suites** (tel. 800/362–2779, www.embassysuites.com). **Fairfield Inn** (tel. 800/228–2800, www.marriott.com). **Four Seasons** (tel. 800/332–3442, www.fourseasons.com). **Hilton** (tel. 800/445–8667, www.hilton.com). **Holiday Inn** (tel. 800/465–4329, www.sixcontinentshotels.com). **Howard Johnson** (tel. 800/654–4656, www.hojo.com). **Hyatt Hotels & Resorts** (tel. 800/233–1234, www.hyatt.com). **Inter-Continental** (tel. 800/327–0200, www.intercontinental.com). **La Quinta** (tel. 800/531–5900, www.laquinta.com). **Marriott** (tel. 800/228–9290, www.marriott.com). **Nikko Hotels International** (tel. 800/645–5687, www.nikkohotels.com). **Omni** (tel. 800/843–6664, www.omnihotels.com). **Quality Inn** (tel. 800/228–5151, www.choicehotels.com). **Radisson** (tel. 800/333–3333, www.radisson.com). **Ramada** (tel. 800/228–2828; 800/854–7854 international reservations; www.ramada.com or www.

ramadahotels.com). **Renaissance Hotels & Resorts** (tel. 800/
468–3571, www.renaissancehotels.com). **Ritz-Carlton** (tel.
800/241–3333, www.ritzcarlton.com). **Sheraton** (tel. 800/325–
3535, www.starwood.com/sheraton). **Sleep Inn** (tel. 800/753–
3746, www.choicehotels.com). **Westin Hotels & Resorts** (tel.
800/228–3000, www.starwood.com/westin).

MOTELS

➤**TOLL-FREE NUMBERS: Econo Lodge** (tel. 800/553–2666).
Hampton Inn (tel. 800/426–7866). **La Quinta** (tel. 800/531–
5900). **Motel 6** (tel. 800/466–8356). **Rodeway** (tel. 800/228–
2000). **Super 8** (tel. 800/848–8888).

Money Matters

Prices throughout this guide are given for adults. Substantially
reduced fees are almost always available for children, students,
and senior citizens. For information on taxes, *see* Taxes, *below.*

CREDIT CARDS

Throughout this guide, the following abbreviations are used:
AE, American Express; **D,** Discover; **DC,** Diners Club; **MC,**
MasterCard; and **V,** Visa.

➤**REPORTING LOST CARDS: American Express** (tel. 800/441–
0519). **Discover** (tel. 800/347–2683). **Diners Club** (tel. 800/
234–6377). **MasterCard** (tel. 800/622–7747). **Visa** (tel. 800/
847–2911).

Packing

Typical of the Southwest, temperatures can vary considerably
from sunup to sundown. You should **pack for warm days and
chilly nights.** In winter pack very warm clothes. And **bring
comfortable shoes;** you're likely to be doing a lot of walking.

New Mexico is one of the most informal and laid-back areas of
the country, which for many is part of its appeal. Casual clothing

is the norm everywhere. The western look has, of course, never lost its hold on the West, though western-style clothes now get mixed with tweed jackets, for example, for a more conservative, sophisticated image. You can wear your boots and big belt buckles in even the best places in Santa Fe and Taos.

Bring skin moisturizer; even people who rarely need this elsewhere in the country can suffer from dry and itchy skin in New Mexico. And **bring sunglasses** to protect your eyes from the glare of lakes or ski slopes. High altitude can cause headaches and dizziness, so check with your doctor about medication to alleviate symptoms. Sunscreen is a necessity. When planning even a short day trip, especially if there's hiking or exercise involved, always pack a bottle or two of water—it's very easy to become dehydrated in New Mexico.

In your carry-on luggage, **pack an extra pair of eyeglasses or contact lenses and enough of any medication** you take to last a few days longer than the entire trip. You may also ask your doctor to write a spare prescription using the drug's generic name, since brand names may vary from country to country. In luggage to be checked, **never pack prescription drugs or valuables.** To avoid customs and security delays, carry medications in their original packaging. Don't pack any sharp objects in your carry-on luggage, including knives of any size or material, scissors, manicure tools, and corkscrews, or anything else that might arouse suspicion. And don't forget to carry with you the addresses of offices that handle refunds of lost traveler's checks. Check *Fodor's How to Pack* (available in bookstores everywhere) for more tips.

CHECKING LUGGAGE

You are allowed one carry-on bag and one personal article, such as a purse or a laptop computer. Make sure that everything you carry aboard will fit under your seat or in the overhead bin. Get to the gate early, so you can board as soon as possible, before the overhead bins fill up.

Before departure, **itemize your bags' contents** and their worth, and label the bags with your name, address, and phone number. (If you use your home address, cover it so potential thieves can't see it readily.) Inside each bag, **pack a copy of your itinerary.** At check-in, **make sure that each bag is correctly tagged** with the destination airport's three-letter code. If your bags arrive damaged or fail to arrive at all, file a written report with the airline before leaving the airport.

Attendants at Albuquerque's airport match your luggage's baggage claim ticket to the number placed on your boarding pass envelope, so **have the envelope handy as you exit the baggage claim area.**

Shopping

Look for antiques, authentic Indian jewelry and handcrafted items, and Mexican goods, like leatherwork and ceramics. You can stock up on western-style clothing and cowboy boots here, too. The Wingspread Collectors Guide compiles useful listings of art galleries throughout the state.

➤**WINGSPREAD GUIDES OF NEW MEXICO, INC.: Wingspread Guides of New Mexico, Inc.** (Box 13566, Albuquerque 87192, tel. 505/292–7537 or 800/873–4278, www.collectorsguide.com).

WATCH OUT

In New Mexico and other southwestern states, shysters marketing fake Indian jewelry and blankets are a continuing problem. Your best guarantee of authenticity, particularly involving Navajo blankets, is to purchase directly from a reputable reservation outlet; the goods sold at the Palace of the Governors in Santa Fe are also all guaranteed handmade by Indian artisans and are high quality. At other shops, **ask for a certificate of authenticity, written verification of a piece's origin, or a receipt** that lists the materials that make up an item. The Indian Arts and Crafts Association offers free information on what to look for in Indian-made goods and sells buyers' guides as well.

➤**INDIAN ARTS AND CRAFTS ASSOCIATION: IACA** (4010 Carlisle NE, Suite C, Santa Fe 87592-9780, tel. 505/265-9149, www.iaca.com).

Sightseeing Tours

FROM SANTA FE

Aboot About has been walking groups through the history, art, and architecture of Santa Fe since the late 1970s. Tours ($10) leave twice daily from the Eldorado Hotel and the Hotel St. Francis. Great Southwest Tours conducts guided mountain hikes and 7- to 35-passenger van and bus excursions to Bandelier, Abiquiu, Taos, and elsewhere in the region; it also provides a shuttle service to and from downtown hotels and the Santa Fe Opera. Santa Fe Detours conducts bus, river, rail, horseback, and walking tours and organizes rafting and ski packages. Rojo Tours designs specialized trips—to view wildflowers, pueblo ruins and cliff dwellings, galleries and studios, Native American arts and crafts, and private homes—as well as adventure activity tours. Afoot in Santa Fe Tours conducts a two-hour close-up look at the city. The tours ($10) leave from the Inn at Loretto from Monday to Sunday at 9:30. Afoot offers open-air trolley tours ($12) several times daily, April–October.

There are also more than 20 independent tour guides based in Santa Fe who are members of the New Mexico Guides Association. Many of these individuals have particular specialties. For example, Kay Lewis's tours emphasize regional art; Stefanie Beninato can give customized ghost, Jewish legacy, or garden walks; Chip Conway's rambles explore the cultures of New Mexico's indigenous peoples, and former Smithsonian docent Barbara Harrelson offers tours that focus on Southwest literature and authors. Other guides specialize in everything from German-language narration to all-women adventures to Georgia O'Keeffe.

➤**TOUR OPERATORS: Aboot About** (tel. 505/988–2774).
Afoot in Santa Fe Tours (tel. 505/983–3701). **Great Southwest Tours** (tel. 505/455–2700, www.swadventures.com). **New Mexico Guides Association** (tel. 505/466–4877, www. nmguides.com/members.html). **Rojo Tours** (tel. 505/474–8333, www.rojotours.com). **Santa Fe Detours** (tel. 505/983–6565 or 800/338–6877, www.sfdetours.com).

FROM TAOS

All Aboard guide service conducts 1¼-hour walking tours in town ($10 per person). Historic Taos Trolley Tours conducts two three-hour narrated tours of Taos daily. Native Sons Adventures organizes biking, backpacking, rafting, snowmobiling, and horseback and wagon expeditions. Roadrunner Tours rents out cars, jeeps, skis, and horses and offers snowmobile tours and sleigh rides from the Elkhorn Lodge near Angel Fire. Taos Indian Horse Ranch conducts two-hour trail rides, as well as old-fashioned horse-drawn sleigh rides through the Taos Pueblo backcountry—winter weather permitting—complete with brass bells, a Native American storyteller, toasted marshmallows, and green-chile roasts. Escorted horseback tours and hayrides are run through Native American lands during the remainder of the year. Taos Studio Tours offers individual or small group tours to galleries and artists' studios, Saturday mornings June–September or by appointment all year.

➤**TOUR OPERATORS: All Aboard** (tel. 505/758–9368). **Historic Taos Trolley Tours** (tel. 505/751–0366, www. taostrolleytours.com). **Native Sons Adventures** (715 Paseo del Pueblo Sur, Taos, tel. 505/758–9342 or 800/753–7559). **Roadrunner Tours** (tel. 505/377–6416). **Taos Indian Horse Ranch** (1 Miller Rd., Taos Pueblo, tel. 800/659–3210). **Taos Pueblo Governor's Office** (tel. 505/758–9593). **Taos Studio Tours** (tel. 505/751–1965, www.taostours.com).

Taxes

SALES TAX

The standard state gross receipts tax rate is 5%, but municipalities and counties enact additional charges at varying rates. Even with additional charges, you will encounter no sales tax higher than 7%.

Taxis

Capital City Cab Company controls all the cabs in Santa Fe. The taxis aren't metered; you pay a flat fee based on how far you're going, usually $4–$8 within the downtown area. There are no cab stands; you must phone to arrange a ride. Taxi service in Taos is sparse, but Faust's Transportation, based in nearby El Prado, has a fleet of radio-dispatched cabs.

➤**CONTACT: Capital City Cab Company** (tel. 505/438–0000). **Faust's Transportation** (tel. 505/758–3410 or 505/758–7359).

Time

New Mexico observes mountain standard time, switching over with most of the rest of the country to daylight saving time in the spring through fall. In New Mexico, you'll be two hours behind New York and one hour ahead of Arizona (except during daylight saving time, which Arizona does not observe) and California.

Tipping

In New Mexico, as elsewhere in the country, a 15%–20% tip is standard for restaurant service.

Tours and Packages

Because everything is prearranged on a prepackaged tour or independent vacation, you spend less time planning—and often get it all at a good price.

BOOKING WITH AN AGENT

Travel agents are excellent resources. But it's a good idea to collect brochures from several agencies, as some agents' suggestions may be influenced by relationships with tour and package firms that reward them for volume sales. If you have a special interest, **find an agent with expertise in that area**; the American Society of Travel Agents (ASTA; ☞ Travel Agencies, *below*) has a database of specialists worldwide.

Make sure your travel agent knows the accommodations and other services of the place being recommended. Has your agent been there in person or sent others whom you can contact? Do some homework on your own, too: local tourism boards can provide information about lesser-known and small-niche operators, some of which may sell only direct.

BUYER BEWARE

Each year consumers are stranded or lose their money when tour operators—even large ones with excellent reputations—go out of business. So **check out the operator**. Ask several travel agents about its reputation, and try to **book with a company that has a consumer-protection program**. (Look for information in the company's brochure.) In the United States, members of the National Tour Association and the United States Tour Operators Association are required to set aside funds to cover your payments and travel arrangements in the event that the company defaults. It's also a good idea to choose a company that participates in the American Society of Travel Agents' Tour Operator Program (TOP); ASTA will act as mediator in any disputes between you and your tour operator.

Remember that the more your package or tour includes the better you can predict the ultimate cost of your vacation. Make sure you know exactly what is covered, and **beware of hidden costs.** Are taxes, tips, and transfers included? Entertainment and excursions? These can add up.

➤**TOUR-OPERATOR RECOMMENDATIONS: American Society of Travel Agents** (☞ Travel Agencies, *below*). **National Tour Association** (NTA; 546 E. Main St., Lexington, KY 40508, tel. 859/226–4444 or 800/682–8886, www.ntaonline.com). **New Mexico Guides Association** (Box 2463, Santa Fe 87504, tel. 505/466–4877, www.nmguides.com). **United States Tour Operators Association** (USTOA; 275 Madison Ave., Suite 2014, New York, NY 10016, tel. 212/599–6599 or 800/468–7862, fax 212/599–6744, www.ustoa.com).

Train Travel

Amtrak's *Southwest Chief*, from Chicago to Los Angeles via Kansas City, stops in Lamy (near Santa Fe) daily.

➤**TRAIN INFORMATION: Amtrak** (tel. 800/872–7245, www.amtrak.com).

Travel Agencies

A good travel agent puts your needs first. Look for an agency that has been in business at least five years, emphasizes customer service, and has someone on staff who specializes in your destination. In addition, **make sure the agency belongs to a professional trade organization.** The American Society of Travel Agents (ASTA)—the largest and most influential in the field with more than 24,000 members in some 140 countries—maintains and enforces a strict code of ethics and will step in to help mediate any agent-client disputes involving ASTA members if necessary. ASTA (whose motto is "Without a travel agent, you're on your own") also maintains a Web site that includes a directory of agents. (If a travel agency is also acting as your tour operator, see Buyer Beware in Tours and Packages, above.)

►**LOCAL AGENT REFERRALS: American Society of Travel Agents** (ASTA; 1101 King St., Suite 200, Alexandria, VA 22314, tel. 800/965–2782 24-hr hot line, fax 703/739–3268, www.astanet.com). **Association of British Travel Agents** (68–71 Newman St., London W1T 3AH, tel. 020/7637–2444, fax 020/7637–0713, www.abtanet.com). **Association of Canadian Travel Agents** (130 Albert St., Suite 1705, Ottawa, Ontario K1P 5G4, tel. 613/237–3657, fax 613/237–7052, www.acta.ca). **Australian Federation of Travel Agents** (Level 3, 309 Pitt St., Sydney, NSW 2000, tel. 02/9264–3299, fax 02/9264–1085, www.afta.com.au). **Travel Agents' Association of New Zealand** (Level 5, Tourism and Travel House, 79 Boulcott St. [Box 1888, Wellington 6001], tel. 04/499–0104, fax 04/499–0827, www.taanz.org.nz).

Visitor Information

For general information before you go, contact the city and state tourism bureaus. If you're interested in learning more about the area's national forests, contact the USDA. For information about Native American attractions, call or visit the Indian Pueblo Cultural Center.

►**CITY INFORMATION: Santa Fe Convention and Visitors Bureau** (201 W. Marcy St., Santa Fe 87501, tel. 505/955–6200 or 800/777–2489, www.santafe.org). **Taos County Chamber of Commerce** (Drawer I, Taos 87571, tel. 505/758–3873 or 800/732–8267, www.taoschamber.com). **Village of Taos Ski Valley Visitors & Conference Bureau** (Box 91, Village of Taos Ski Valley 87525, tel. 800/992–7669, www.skitaos.org or www.taosskivalley.com).

►**STATEWIDE INFORMATION: New Mexico Department of Tourism** (491 Old Santa Fe Trail, Santa Fe 87503, tel. 505/827–7400 or 800/733–6396 ext. 0643, www.newmexico.org).

➤**NATIVE ATTRACTIONS: Indian Pueblo Cultural Center**
(2401 12th St. NW, Albuquerque 87102, tel. 505/843–7270;
800/766–4405 outside New Mexico; www.indianpueblo.org).

Web Sites

Do check out the World Wide Web when planning your trip.
You'll find everything from weather forecasts to virtual tours of
famous cities. Be sure to **visit Fodors.com** (www.fodors.com), a
complete travel-planning site. You can research prices and book
plane tickets, hotel rooms, rental cars, vacation packages, and
more. In addition, you can post your pressing questions in the
"Travel Talk" section. Other planning tools include a currency
converter and weather reports, and there are loads of links to
travel resources.

When to Go

Most ceremonial dances at the Native American pueblos occur
in the summer, early fall, and at Christmas and Easter. The
majority of other major events—including the Santa Fe Opera,
Chamber Music Festival, and Indian and Spanish markets—are
geared to the traditionally heavy tourist season of July and
August. The Santa Fe Fiesta is held in September.

The relatively cool climates of Santa Fe and Taos are a lure in
summer, as is the skiing in Taos and Santa Fe in winter. During
the Christmas season Santa Fe is at its most festive, with incense
and piñon smoke sweetening the air and the darkness of winter
illuminated by thousands of farolitos. A custom believed to have
derived from Chinese lanterns, the glowing paper-bag lanterns
are everywhere, lining walkways, doorways, rooftops, walls, and
window sills. The songs of Christmas are sung around corner
bonfires (luminarias, as the holiday bonfires are called in Santa
Fe). With glowing lights reflected on the snow, Santa Fe is never
lovelier.

Smart Sightseeings

Savvy travelers and others who take their sightseeing seriously have skills worth knowing about.

DON'T PLAN YOUR VISIT IN YOUR HOTEL ROOM Don't wait until you pull into town to decide how to spend your days. It's inevitable that there will be much more to see and do than you'll have time for: choose sights in advance.

ORGANIZE YOUR TOURING Note the places that most interest you on a map, and visit places that are near each other during the same morning or afternoon.

START THE DAY WELL EQUIPPED Leave your hotel in the morning with everything you need for the day—maps, medicines, extra film, your guidebook, rain gear, and another layer of clothing in case the weather turns cooler.

TOUR MUSEUMS EARLY If you're there when the doors open you'll have an intimate experience of the collection.

EASY DOES IT See museums in the mornings, when you're fresh, and visit sit-down attractions later on. Take breaks before you need them.

STRIKE UP A CONVERSATION Only curmudgeons don't respond to a smile and a polite request for information. Most people appreciate your interest in their home town. And your conversations may end up being your most vivid memories.

GET LOST When you do, you never know what you'll find—but you can count on it being memorable. Use your guidebook to help you get back on track. Build wandering-around time into every day.

QUIT BEFORE YOU'RE TIRED There's no point in seeing that one extra sight if you're too exhausted to enjoy it.

TAKE YOUR MOTHER'S ADVICE Go to the bathroom when you have the chance. You never know what lies ahead.

Hotel rates are generally highest during the peak summer season but fluctuate less than those in most major resort areas. If you plan to come in summer, **be sure to make reservations in advance.**

➤**FORECASTS: Weather Channel Connection** (tel. 900/932–8437), 95¢ per minute from a Touch-Tone phone.

The following are average daily maximum and minimum temperatures for Santa Fe.

SANTA FE

Jan.	39F	4C	May	68F	20C	Sept.	73F	23C
	19	-7		42	6		48	9
Feb.	42F	6C	June	78F	26C	Oct.	62F	17C
	23	-5		51	11		37	3
Mar.	51F	11C	July	80F	27C	Nov.	50F	10C
	28	-2		57	14		28	-2
Apr.	59F	15C	Aug.	78F	26C	Dec.	39F	4C
	35	2		55	13		19	-7

GLOSSARY

Perhaps more than any other region in the United States, New Mexico has its own distinctive cuisine and architectural style, both heavily influenced by Native American, Spanish-colonial, Mexican, and American frontier traditions. The brief glossary that follows explains terms frequently used in this book. As befits a land occupied by so many diverse peoples, the use of accents on place and other names is a tricky matter. For some people, among them many Hispanic residents, accents are a matter of identification and pride. On the other hand, though including the accent for Picurís Pueblo or Jémez Pueblo might be linguistically accurate, it's also a reminder of the Spanish conquest of Pueblo Native Americans. ("I couldn't care less whether you use accents or not—I don't," said a woman at the governor's office of Jemez Pueblo when asked whether having an accent above the first "e" in the pueblo's name would be more accurate.)

In general in this book we've applied accents when they're part of an official place or other name. Signs for and official documents of Española, for instance, tend to have a tilde above the "n" in the city's name. On the other hand, though the names of Capulin Volcano and the city of Raton are sometimes written Capulín Volcano and Ratón, we have not employed the accents because New Mexicans rarely do. A generally workable solution, this strategy does lead to some apparent inconsistencies (Picurís Pueblo; Jemez Pueblo), an illustration of the conflicting cultural sentiments still at play within New Mexico.

ART AND ARCHITECTURE

Adobe: A brick of sun-dried earth and clay, usually stabilized with straw; a structure made of adobe.

Banco: A small bench, or banquette, often upholstered with handwoven textiles, that gracefully emerges from adobe walls.

Bulto: Folk-art figures of a santo (saint), usually carved from wood.

Camposanto: A graveyard.

Capilla: A chapel.

Casita: Literally "small house," this term is generally used to describe a separate guest house.

Cerquita: A spiked, wrought-iron, rectangular fence, often marking grave sites.

Corbel: An ornately carved, decorative wooden bracket set between posts and beams.

Coyote fence: A type of wooden fence that surrounds many New Mexico homes; it comprises branches, usually from cedar or aspen trees, arranged vertically and wired tightly together.

Equipal: Pigskin-and-cedar furniture from Jalisco, Mexico, these chairs have rounded backs and bases rather than legs.

Farolito: Small votive candles set in paper-bag lanterns, farolitas are popular at Christmastime. The term is used in northern New Mexico only. People in Albuquerque and points south call the lanterns *luminarias*, which in the north is the term for the bonfires of Christmas Eve.

Heishi: Shell jewelry.

Hornos: Outdoor domed ovens.

Kiva: A ceremonial room, rounded and built at least partially underground, used by Native Americans of the Southwest. Entrance is gained from the roof.

Kiva fireplace: A corner fireplace whose round form resembles that of a kiva.

Latilla: Small pole, often made of aspen, used as a lath in a ceiling.

Nicho: A built-in shelf cut into an adobe or stucco wall.

Placita: A small plaza.

Portal: A porch or large covered area adjacent to a house.

Pueblo Revival (also informally called Pueblo-style): Most homes in this style, modeled after the traditional dwellings of the Southwest Pueblo Indians, are cube or rectangle shaped. Other characteristics are flat roofs, thick adobe or stucco walls, small windows, rounded corners, and viga beams.

Retablo: Holy image painted on wood or tin.

Santero: Maker of religious images.

Territorial style: This modified Pueblo style evolved in the late 19th century when New Mexico was still a U.S. territory. The Territorial home incorporates a broad central hallway and entryway and adds wooden elements, such as window frames, in neoclassical style; some structures have pitched (often corrugated or flat metal) rather than flat roofs, and brick copings.

Terrones adobes: Adobe cut from the ground rather than formed from mud.

Viga: Horizontal roof beam made of logs, usually protruding from the side of the house.

MENU GUIDE

Aguacate: Spanish for avocado, the key ingredient of guacamole.

Albóndigas: Meatballs, usually cooked with rice in a meat broth.

Bolsa del pobre: A seafood and vegetable dish; a specialty from Colima.

Burrito: A warm flour tortilla wrapped around meat, beans, and vegetables and smothered in chile and cheese; many New Mexicans also love breakfast burritos (filled with any combination of the above, along with eggs).

Carne adovada: Red chile–marinated pork.

Chalupa: A corn tortilla deep-fried in the shape of a bowl, filled with pinto beans (sometimes meat), and topped with cheese, guacamole, sour cream, lettuce, tomatoes, and salsa.

Chilaquiles: Often served at breakfast, this casserole-like dish consists of small pieces of fried tortillas baked with red or green chiles, bits of chicken or cheese, and sometimes eggs.

Chile RELLENO: A large green chile pepper peeled, stuffed with cheese or a special mixture of spicy ingredients, dipped in batter, and fried.

Chiles: New Mexico's infamous hot peppers, which come in an endless variety of sizes and in various degrees of hotness, from the thumb-size jalapeño to the smaller and often hotter serrano. They can be canned or fresh, dried or cut up into salsa. Most traditional New Mexican dishes are served either with green, red, or both types of chiles (ask for "Christmas" when indicating to your server that you'd like both red and green). Famous regional uses for green chile include green chile stew (usually made with shredded pork), green chile cheeseburgers, and green chile–and–cheese tamales.

Chili: A stewlike dish with Texas origins that typically contains beans, beef, and red chile.

Chimichanga: The same as a burrito (☞ *above*), only deep-fried and topped with a dab of sour cream or salsa. (The chimichanga was invented in Tucson, Arizona.)

Chipotle: A dried smoked jalapeño with a smoky, almost sweet, chocolaty flavor.

Chorizo: Well-spiced Spanish sausage, made with pork and red chiles.

Enchilada: A rolled or flat corn tortilla filled with meat, chicken, seafood, or cheese, an enchilada is covered with chile and baked. The ultimate enchilada is made with blue Indian corn tortillas. New Mexicans order them flat, sometimes topped with a fried egg.

Fajitas: A Tex-Mex dish of grilled beef, chicken, fish, or roasted vegetables and served with peppers, onions, and pico de gallo, served with tortillas; traditionally known as arracheras.

Flauta: A tortilla filled with cheese or meat and rolled into a flutelike shape ("flauta" means flute) and lightly fried.

Frijoles refritos: Refried beans, often seasoned with lard or cheese.

Guacamole: Mashed avocado, mixed with tomatoes, garlic, onions, lemon juice, and chiles, used as a dip, a side dish, a topping, or an additional ingredient.

Hatch: A small southern New Mexico town in the Mesilla Valley, known for its outstanding production and quality of both green and red chile. The "Hatch" name often is found on canned chile food products.

Huevos rancheros: New Mexico's answer to eggs Benedict—eggs doused with chile and sometimes melted cheese, served on top of a corn tortilla (they're good accompanied by chorizo).

Pan de cazón: Grilled shark with black beans and red onions on a tortilla; a specialty from Campeche.

Posole: Resembling popcorn soup, this is a sublime marriage of lime, hominy, pork, chile, garlic, and spices.

Quesadilla: A folded flour tortilla filled with cheese and meat or vegetables and warmed or lightly fried so the cheese melts.

Queso: Cheese; an ingredient in many Mexican and southwestern recipes (cheddar or jack is used most commonly in New Mexican dishes).

Ristra: String of dried red chile peppers, often used as decoration.

Salsa: Finely chopped concoction of green and red chile peppers, mixed with onion, garlic, and other spices.

Sopaipilla: Puffy deep-fried bread that's similar to Navajo fry bread (found in Arizona and western New Mexico); it's served either as a dessert with honey drizzled over it or savory as a meal stuffed with pinto beans or meat.

Taco: A corn or flour tortilla served either soft, or baked or fried and served in a hard shell; it's then stuffed with vegetables or spicy meat and garnished with shredded lettuce, chopped tomatoes, onions, and grated cheese.

Tacos al carbón: Shredded pork cooked in a mole sauce and folded into corn tortillas.

Tamale: Ground corn made into a dough, often filled with finely ground pork and red chiles; it's steamed in a corn husk.

Tortilla: A thin pancake made of corn or wheat flour, a tortilla is used as bread, as an edible "spoon," and as a container for other foods. Locals place butter in the center of a hot tortilla, roll it up, and eat it as a scroll.

Trucha en terra-cotta: Fresh trout wrapped in corn husks and baked in clay.

Verde: Spanish for "green," as in chile verde (a green chile sauce).

index

Fodor's
Key to the Guides

America's guidebook leader publishes guides for every kind of traveler. Check out our many series and find your perfect match.

Fodor's Gold Guides
America's favorite travel-guide series offers the most detailed insider reviews of hotels, restaurants, and attractions in all price ranges, plus great background information, smart tips, and useful maps.

Fodor's Road Guide USA
Big guides for a big country—the most comprehensive guides to America's roads, packed with places to stay, eat, and play across the U.S.A. Just right for road warriors, family vacationers, and cross-country trekkers.

COMPASS AMERICAN GUIDES
Stunning guides from top local writers and photographers, with gorgeous photos, literary excerpts, and colorful anecdotes. A must-have for culture mavens, history buffs, and new residents.

Fodor's CITYPACKS
Concise city coverage with a foldout map. The right choice for urban travelers who want everything under one cover.

Fodor's EXPLORING GUIDES
Hundreds of color photos bring your destination to life. Lively stories lend insight into the culture, history, and people.

Fodor's POCKET GUIDES
For travelers who need only the essentials. The best of Fodor's in pocket-size packages for just $9.95.

Fodor's To Go
Credit-card–size, magnetized color microguides that fit in the palm of your hand—perfect for "stealth" travelers or as gifts.

Fodor's FLASHMAPS
Every resident's map guide. 60 easy-to-follow maps of public transit, parks, museums, zip codes, and more.

Fodor's CITYGUIDES
Sourcebooks for living in the city: Thousands of in-the-know listings for restaurants, shops, sports, nightlife, and other city resources.

Fodor's AROUND THE CITY WITH KIDS
68 great ideas for family days, recommended by resident parents. Perfect for exploring in your own backyard or on the road.

Fodor's ESCAPES
Fill your trip with once-in-a-lifetime experiences, from ballooning in Chianti to overnighting in the Moroccan desert. These full-color dream books point the way.

Fodor's FYI
Get tips from the pros on planning the perfect trip. Learn how to pack, fly hassle-free, plan a honeymoon or cruise, stay healthy on the road, and travel with your baby.

Fodor's Languages for Travelers
Practice the local language before hitting the road. Available in phrase books, cassette sets, and CD sets.

Karen Brown's Guides
Engaging guides to the most charming inns and B&Bs in the U.S.A. and Europe, with easy-to-follow inn-to-inn itineraries.

Baedeker's Guides
Comprehensive guides, trusted since 1829, packed with A–Z reviews and star ratings.

FODOR'S POCKET SANTA FE AND TAOS

EDITORS: Constance Jones and Emmanuelle Morgen

Editorial Contributors: Andrew Collins, Holly Hammond

Editorial Production: David Downing

Maps: David Lindroth, *cartographer*; Bob Blake and Rebecca Baer, *map editors*

Design: Fabrizio La Rocca, *creative director*; Tigist Getachew, *art director*; Jolie Novak, *senior picture editor*; Melanie Marin, *photo editor*

Production/Manufacturing: Angela L.McLean

Cover Photograph: Corbis

Third Edition

ISBN 1–4000–1122–1

ISSN 1534–1372

IMPORTANT TIP

Although all prices, opening times, and other details in this book are based on information supplied to us at press time, changes occur all the time in the travel world, and Fodor's cannot accept responsibility for facts that become outdated or for inadvertent errors or omissions. So **always confirm information when it matters,** especially if you're making a detour to visit a specific place.

SPECIAL SALES

Fodor's Travel Publications are available at special discounts for bulk purchases for sales promotions or premiums. Special editions, including personalized covers, excerpts of existing guides, and corporate imprints, can be created in large quantities for special needs. For more information, contact your local bookseller or write to Special Markets, Fodor's Travel Publications, 1745 Broadway, New York, NY 10019. Inquiries from Canada should be directed to your local Canadian bookseller or sent to Random House of Canada, Ltd., Marketing Department, 2775 Matheson Boulevard East, Mississauga, Ontario L4W 4P7. Inquiries from the United Kingdom should be sent to Fodor's Travel Publications, 20 Vauxhall Bridge Road, London SW1V 2SA, England.

PRINTED IN THE UNITED STATES OF AMERICA

10 9 8 7 6 5 4 3 2 1